UBERTHERAPY
The New Business of Mental Health

Elizabeth Cotton

First published in Great Britain in 2025 by
Bristol University Press
University of Bristol
1–9 Old Park Hill
Bristol
BS2 8BB
UK
t: +44 (0)117 374 6645
e: bup-info@bristol.ac.uk

Details of international sales and distribution partners are available at bristoluniversitypress.co.uk

© Bristol University Press 2025

DOI: 10.51952/9781529230857

British Library Cataloguing in Publication Data
A catalogue record for this book is available from the British Library

ISBN 978-1-5292-3082-6 hardcover
ISBN 978-1-5292-3083-3 paperback
ISBN 978-1-5292-3084-0 ePub
ISBN 978-1-5292-3085-7 ePdf

The right of Elizabeth Cotton to be identified as author of this work has been asserted by her in accordance with the Copyright, Designs and Patents Act 1988.

All rights reserved: no part of this publication may be reproduced, stored in a retrieval system, or transmitted in any form or by any means, electronic, mechanical, photocopying, recording, or otherwise without the prior permission of Bristol University Press.

Every reasonable effort has been made to obtain permission to reproduce copyrighted material. If, however, anyone knows of an oversight, please contact the publisher.

The statements and opinions contained within this publication are solely those of the author and not of the University of Bristol or Bristol University Press. The University of Bristol and Bristol University Press disclaim responsibility for any injury to persons or property resulting from any material published in this publication.

Bristol University Press and Policy Press work to counter discrimination on grounds of gender, race, disability, age and sexuality.

Cover design: Gareth Davies
Front cover image: Stocksy / Oleksandra Stets

For my son

Contents

Prologue		vii
1	**Angerland**	**1**
	Welcome to Angerland	1
	Hi Sigmund™	3
	The therapeutic Wild West	6
	Size matters	9
	The datafication of despair	11
	Sabor a Mierda	13
	Defences against thinking	16
2	**UberTherapy**	**20**
	The architecture of UberTherapy	20
	It's always all about sex	21
	UberTherapists	28
	Attrition by design	31
	Self-regulation	32
3	**Psychic Pilates**	**37**
	The IAPT juggernaut	38
	Hello from the therapy factory	41
	SilverLinings	45
	Cheer up love	49
	Is something better than nothing?	51
4	**Do You Have to Marry a Rich Man to Be a Therapist?**	**53**
	In Versailles	53
	The Grand Commun	55
	Wage theft and predatory pricing	58
	Professional cannibalism	62
	Guillotine logic	65

5	**Therapeutic Tinder**	**68**
	Don't get defensive	68
	Look. At. Me.	69
	Retail therapy	71
	MILF therapy	73
	Revenge therapy	74
	Harder than you think is a beautiful thing	76
6	***RealTherapy*™**	**80**
	Dirty little ideological secrets	80
	Lived experience	85
	Social intentions	86
	The intention of free association	87
	The intention to think	90
	The intention to face reality	95
	The intention of AI-MHS	97
	MuchBetterHelp	99
	Stop dancing for daddy	102
References		106
Index		129

Prologue

UberTherapy comes from the knowledge that I have become dangerously tired of having things explained to me by people who do not live it, and now that I know that about myself it makes space for me to be more intentional about what and how I write. My intention is not to shame anyone who uses therapy apps or works for a therapy platform. My intention is to provide some useful ideas for navigating the new business of mental health on both sides of the therapeutic relationship. As a result, this book is written in a language and style geared towards anyone with skin in the therapy game.

UberTherapy was imagined during the pandemic and written in the fallout years. Part of me and all of my publisher wishes it had been written earlier to capitalize on the artificial intelligence (AI) media frenzy that exploded in 2023. But as a single parent to a one year old when lockdown happened I did not spend the pandemic writing a book, just two years staring into the abyss of mental distress and rethinking my well-rehearsed narratives about survival. Post-it notes littered my transient homes, intense serial killer scribbles in journals, burner phones and made-up identities for my deep dive into AI wellbeing tools. Just before lockdown I got a new job while on maternity leave and I went to my first meeting with my actual baby, all of us puffed up that the world had changed so much that the walls did not fall in. Towards the end of a collegial meeting of the kind promoted by the presence of pets and kids I noticed my baby was flirting wildly across the room with a young woman from Human Resources. Smiles and giggles, shouting and farting, him not her. She suddenly burst into tears and said 'I'm sorry, I'd forgotten what it feels like to be so liked by someone'. I ache when I think about that moment when the penny dropped that my entire universe had now shifted towards the what-it-feels-like to be loved. That my internal architecture reflected a new axis and the immediate sinking feeling that this was going to end my career.

I am not going to argue that you have to be a parent to care about AI, but caring deeply for another person intensified deeply my response to those services that no longer serve. I wonder if I will ever recover from the months of child-care-free working life, of isolation and anxiety, watching the data roll in about women's job loss as my academic colleagues wrote about my inequalities. All that *TotalRecovery* advertising about the power of short-term therapy to manage my negative cognitions and bad behaviours while walking the everyday tightrope of quarantine to the nauseating point of overwhelm. It is fair to say that during the pandemic I lived a life that I witnessed women bearing in my rural childhood. As the sexism and misogyny women thinkers now face returns us to Sunday lunch in rural south-west England in the 1970s, we whisper stories from our domestic enclosures, eyes to the floor ashamed. We quietly ask do you feel it too?

I wrote this book in the voice of my online character Surviving Work[1] and its body of work about therapy as a labour process and an emancipatory process of growth. Surviving Work was always about my failed attempts to do just that, coming out of my experience of finding myself in a compulsory redundancy pool for the first time in my life somewhere in 2011. After a career working in global unions and with trade unions in the extractive industries, defending others' rights, within just a few years of becoming a professional person I realized I was not in a fit state to even defend myself. My ego could not manage my own emerging redundancy, which triggered an existential crisis I should have had several years earlier while working with unions in Colombia (Cotton and Royle, 2015) and Azerbaijan (Croucher and Cotton, 2011). Like most activists I had for too long existed in that dangerous place between love and hate where betrayal and burnout make even the best of us mean. This process of my breaking down was supported by nine years of psychoanalysis which, in its honest and gruesome precision, gave me the cosmic shove I needed to drop the heroics and try to be myself.

Drawing on my experience of adult education and socially engaged research under the title Surviving Work, I carried out a series of large surveys of therapists, counsellors and mental health workers – much of this has been published, all of it used online and in partnership with progressive actors in therapy to promote debate about the strategic uberization of mental health services in the UK, most recently in a collaborative body of work The Digital Therapy Project.[2] Surviving Work is based on the principles of critical action learning (CAL) in that it adopts a critical perspective and examines power relations, explores emotional experience and is action oriented (Cotton, 2021). This model of emancipatory education that dominates trade union organizing privileges an ontology based on the work of Paulo Freire (Freire, 1970) and the intention to find methods that can build solidaristic relationships (Cotton, 2017). As such, Surviving Work is a recognized critical space for people engaged in therapeutic work (Cotton, 2019) which in part explains the reach and engagement of the data referenced here that includes unusually high numbers of UberTherapists – the growing majority of mental health practitioners who work in non-clinical and generic roles, often unwaged or on low pay, presenting a reality that is both under-articulated and under-theorized in what we know about the therapy factory. It is the reason why some of the claims and ideas in this book might be hard for you to swallow because it represents the underbelly of what happens when the professions are platformized.

It was not until I read Kate Crawford's (2021) phenomenal mapping of the material realities of AI that I understood the connection between my experiences of the mining and the therapy sectors and how they combined in the new business model of UberTherapy. Whether it is about patient data, rare earth elements or digiceuticals, the business model is founded on a fundamental extraction of something of value and the deep exploitation of workers this inevitably involves. It explains why UberTherapy in a way has nothing to do with therapy, and why the everyday extraction of therapeutic data, to use or sell on to build more AI diagnostic tools and promote consumption of corporatized care, has come to be, and how until you are in it, you do not see what is wrong with this new business of mental health.

The idea of UberTherapy has been taken up by the media (Wiseman, 2021) and the interest in therapy chatbots that started post-COVID as the automation of the therapeutic relationship became a literal reality. Some of the best books referenced here are written by journalists writing with a freedom that no longer exists for many academics needing to evidence their research excellence. The importance of the media and independent journalism in setting safeguards around this new business model should not be underestimated as much of the progress being made to challenge uberization is done by protecting the rights of the consumers through bringing the risks to our attention in a highly competitive attention market. This has started a litigious front line to the therapy debates – where consumer rights, anti-competition legislation and advertising standards are starting to shape the fault lines of 'responsible business'. The concerns about UberTherapy are translating into a tide of consumer complaints about individual therapists and the very personal attacks on them that a depressing search of social media and chatrooms reveals. This engagement with journalists and the media continues to be important as we navigate this new corporate architecture and formulate an idea of AI-Mental Health and Safety (AI-MHS).

This book exists at the intersection of these experiences of trade unions, of being a sociologist working in academia, of having worked as a therapist and of having had a lot of therapy. Intentionally, throughout this book I have used my experience of what is happening on all four levels because to really understand UberTherapy requires not just describing and analysing it but also the blood and guts of how that makes us feel. A psychoanalytic framework is useful here because it pays attention to unconscious and psychic phenomena such as projection and splitting exhibited in workplace settings (Obholzer and Zagier Roberts, 2019), and gives priority to the 'emotional vocabulary' (Durnova, 2024) of therapeutic workers. It allows us to talk about and think about UberTherapy from different and deeply personal perspectives, raising our consciousness and unconsciousness in parallel.

There are no self-reporting questionnaires that allow us to think about UberTherapy precisely because the metrics of recovery were created to capture industrially useful information and to avoid, by design, critical thinking. It means that to go deep into what the problem is with UberTherapy requires what Nora Bateson (2022) calls 'information of another order' that symbolizes the warm data of experience. Throughout this book, a character I call Hair-n-Teeth is used to capture that information of another order. Passages of the book that are in the voice of Hair-n-Teeth are indicated by the use of vertical lines on either side of the text. This is my internal cave dweller who I live with and am on acceptable terms with thanks to a lot of therapy. It is the part of me that has experienced trauma, wasn't able to speak about that and buried it until I couldn't. It is the part of me that sleeps in a psychic cave, its fur tunic on, with a club close to hand, that I have to switch off when I pick my child up from school. The part who fears that the literal and symbolic parents-who-don't-parent will notice their shame and project it forward across the next generation so that it can never be owned and worked through. It is the part of me that runs the battery of my political mind, that has a problem with authority and knows without any doubt that we already live under a fascistic logic now automated in the everyday. I did not know when I started this book that so much of it would be about shame and anger but it was, and Hair-n-Teeth offers a perspective for measuring the real embodied algorithmic harms and a place to resist a system that asks us to stay calm when we cannot nor should not.

Hair-n-Teeth gave me a way of understanding the blaming of the individual in need of care by a system designed to override human needs, what I call in this book neoliberal paternalism, and it is for this reason that I unexpectedly wrote a distinctly feminist book. The appeal to warm data is a call for us to re-embody therapeutic work and raise our consciousness of its degradation through uberization. Drawing on our personal and embodied experiences as a route to raising consciousness, is a deeply feminist basis for research. It is a positioning that values the subjectivity of the author, that values experience and recognizes the difference that lived experience makes to the accuracy and legitimacy of the argument.

Part of my privilege is that I am a native speaker of English, which means that I am often too confident in my belief that I do not need AI technologies to write a book, although they have become so embedded in our systems of work that it is hard to imagine any AI-free labour process. Despite this privilege of language, I have spent much of my intellectual and political life being described as superficial because of the radicalism-lite tone of my writing, and finally in my middle age I do not consider that to be fair. I wanted to say that out loud as people have started to call me brave which so easily slips into calling me stupid. As a woman I love, who has over-achieved for her entire life recently said to me, 'COVID-19 has taught me that I just can't keep auditioning for a place in my own life'. That is why this book is also a feminist love letter that prioritizes the intellectual work of women and feminist men and that understands the value of talking from experience. It is in this spirit that I have included in this book the exceptional thinkers and practitioners who have changed me. I attempted to decolonize my own theoretical framing, bought and then actually read new writings and excluded those usual suspects in my fields who have ethical or political form. For those activists among you, it will not shock you horribly to know that just because someone writes about solidarity does not mean that in any way they are able to live it graciously in the real. There is also intentionally a large volume of endnotes, news and articles about digital therapy, reflecting the key role of journalists and 'algoactivists' (van Toorn, 2024) in tracking platform capitalism, and subsequently a key part of the evidence for the arguments laid out here.

In the final months before publication I was encouraged to sit with my book and to allow my authority to speak up, giving me time to reflect on the nature of seeing things before others. An occupational hazard for writers is to bask in our ahead-of-time thinking when anyone with any political experience knows that to be right first is a hollow victory. Therapists understand profoundly the risk of talking about something that people are defended against seeing, and how by seeing the problem you can become the problem. If you have ever been on strike you will also hold the bitter knowledge that being right is not enough and that what matters most is being right at a time when people are ready to hear it and ready to use it in their lives. As the myths and monsters of AI become mainstreamed into our culture I no longer fear that the book will be out of date before it hits the shelves, because the best outcome is that you read it at a time when you have had enough stories about Tech Titans in immortal combat and you are ready to think ahead about where you place yourself in the future algorithmic landscape. When we are not stuck in the whatabouts and whatifs of technology taken out of context, and ready to do the depressive work of understanding the financial and digital systems that we are now working in, sufficient to resist their logical conclusions.

Hundreds of years ago when I thought I had a place in the world of digital health I tried to get fresh start-up funding for an app called *Angerland: Punching and spitting your way to wellbeing at work*. Genuinely, there was a year or so when I believed in the radical potential of smartphones in finding a progressive and protected space where we could talk honestly about mental health at work. As someone who bought into the early years of cyber campaigning for international solidarity and came out the other side, I do not underestimate the connectivity that the internet and social media has given us. But I also know that built into the technology is the drive to self-replicate such that the economic and industrial systems behind it are only ever reinforced. Ultimately the algorithm never radicalizes until we tell it to.

I argue in this book that the business case for UberTherapy rests on a disdain for complexity, of vulnerability and knowing a reality that many online platforms and policy makers are in the business of denying where there are no magic solutions to our mental distress. Two things you should be alert to in the debates about digital therapy that we try to unpack in this book are whose interests are these stories serving and what are their intentions. The proposed therapeutic litmus test used in this book is whether digital therapies can help you to sit alongside those parts of yourself that need healing long enough to accept the facts of your life. Not to be gaslit into thinking it is our fault or to be nudged into giving up on other people, instead asking whether digital therapy allows us to relate in a way that we can reasonably consent to and that is healthy and safe from the augmented potential for self-harm. As part of this protection of the therapeutic framework, this book argues that a parallel protection of therapists needs to take place and for this to happen we need to understand the interlock between human rights and workers' rights. When we are ready to understand that free association requires freedom of association.

The structure of this book is to look at the characteristics of UberTherapy, how we got here and where we might go next. Chapter 1, Angerland, gives an overview of the disorienting AI industry and how digital therapy acts as a defence against thinking about reality. Chapter 2, UberTherapy, gives an overview of the business models of digital therapy and the uberization process that has taken place involving the industrialization and the de-industrialization of therapeutic work. Chapter 3, Psychic Pilates, looks at the uberization of therapy that took place under the UK's largest public mental health programme in the NHS, and the gamification of recovery across the therapy sector. It explores the impact of introducing an existential crisis into therapy that questions both its principles and practices through the introduction of cognitive behavioural therapy (CBT) 'lite' (CBT-Lite) and its digital form iCBT-Lite. Chapter 4, Do You Have to Marry a Rich Man to Be a Therapist?, looks at the data around wage theft in the therapy sector and the cannibalistic nature of the professional landscape and the 'guillotine logic' that underpins it. Chapter 5, Therapeutic Tinder, looks at what happens to our therapeutic relationships when they move online and are mediated by online platforms and social media. It looks at how the business model shapes the therapeutic relationship using ideas of MILF therapy and the link to the Oedipus Complex, Retail Therapy and dynamic pricing and Revenge Therapy as a way of avoiding the fact of life that we are dependent on other people. Chapter 6, *RealTherapy*™, tries to imagine a better model of therapy and explores areas of intentional work that are worth our time and energy, offering a breadcrumb trail out of Angerland towards a MuchBetterHelp. It argues for the intention of freedom of association, of facing up to the trauma of work and the existence of work-related suicide, the intention to think critically and an intention to establish an AI-MHS for both therapists and their clients. Finally, it argues for the intention to resist and remove those technologies that act as a defence against thinking and to allow ourselves to rethink the new business of mental health.

I have not named anyone or any corporation in the writing of this book. Partly to avoid being sued, partly to avoid putting people I care about on a radical hit list. One of the very many worthwhile things about having had real therapy is that it taught me how to have confidence in my ability to love, so those of you who have been part of the development of me and this book already know it. It is in our free associations that this book became a love letter about how it is that other people are not a waste of time.

Notes

1. Surviving Work, www.survivingwork.org
2. The Digital Therapy Project, www.thedigitaltherapyproject.org

1

Angerland

Welcome to Angerland

After a decade of researching the therapy industry I have finally formulated the elevator pitch for UberTherapy – 'The Datafication of Despair: The extraction industry that games reality and offers magic solutions to the problems you never had'. I am supposed to feel happier than this.

The occupational hazard of researching UberTherapy is the rising panic at the size and speed of the uberization process taking place in the therapy sector. I have the feeling of being hurled around on a fairground ride, between the audacious game that is being played with our mental health and what I have come to see as the corrupted intention behind it. The dizzy and disorienting feeling that the ride is about to crash and burn as I race to write this down before the delinquent teenagers in charge of the therapy rollercoasters slam on the brakes and hurl us dangerously in the wrong psychic direction. Watching indifferently as we scream 'go-faster-go-faster-no-stop', smoking cigarettes and chatting up girls without a responsible adult in sight.

As the exaggerated claims of digital health technologies become absorbed into our culture, I find myself in a hall of mirrors, distorted by an idea of therapy I know not to be true offering therapeutic unicorns and guaranteed recovery from being myself. Looking into the digital mirror I wonder at whether I am having an AI hallucination where the therapy Large Language Models (LLMs) and their generative AI (GenAI) offer an instant way out of seeing myself as I really am. A digital Rorschach Test[1] that misinterprets me by joining my biometric ink dots into a pattern that does not, psychically speaking, exist. As they churn out nonsense-making diagnoses and interpretations, my memories of the psychic facts of my life start to fade, where correlation replaces causation in the story of my life. I have the sickening feeling of being sat at the top of a broken Ferris wheel, excited by the panoramic view but without a clue how to get down to the ground safely, deregulated by the thuggish neglectful violence of the system I now see in Angerland.

UberTherapy is a rapidly expanding business model of on-demand and pay-as-you-go mental health care that comes out of a sustained period of industrialization of therapy (Cotton, 2018) and its subsequent deindustrialization through platformization. Although UberTherapy offers a smorgasbord of therapeutic products, in reality it is paradoxically instrumental in securing the domination of cognitive behavioural therapy (CBT) 'lite' – what I call in this book CBT-Lite and its digital manifestation iCBT-Lite – as the therapy of choice in the UK's National Health Service (NHS) and private health insurance sector. CBT-Lite as a short-term, solution-focused and standardized model of therapy that has established an 'evidence base' that recognizes its return on investment (ROI) and its affordability both legally in compliance with The Affordable Care and Patient Protection Act in the US (Lazar, 2023) and clinically such as with the National Institute for Clinical Excellence (NICE) in the UK. CBT-Lite is digitalized into iCBT-Lite, routinely using AI technologies such as chatbots augmented with text-based and guided self-help through the explosion of private medical insurance that comes of a collapsed NHS (Kollewe, 2024). Reinvented through platformization which places us in a therapeutic 'antitrust paradox' (Mattioli, 2024) where you can have everything you want as long as it is iCBT-Lite.

UberTherapy is a granular story of how therapy was uberized through the interlocked processes of marketization (running healthcare on the basis of a financial logic open to the market), commodification (the valuing of patient data and redefining healthcare as a commodity that has to be paid for, on demand, by consumers), standardization (manualizing and creating a one-size-fits-all model of care) and then inevitably the commodification of therapy this allows (where therapy became something that gets bought, by consumers not clients). This allows for cheaper therapy, and opens the door to digitalization and AI technologies in order to automate care. No need to pay a robot or care about their working conditions, no AI trade unions to bang on about the cost of living crisis, and anyone with a professional problem with that can go quietly into private practice.

COVID-19 accelerated something that was already happening, an uberization of care through the interlocked processes of digitalization, platformization, appification and then datafication. Psychotherapy had already started to understand the potential for AI technologies in the US in the 1960s with Joseph Winzenbaum's Eliza experiments that piloted the therapeutic potential of therapy chatbots (Zeavin, 2021). Under UberTherapy the next generation of therapeutic technologies were being piloted during COVID-19, and giving out our biometric data became normalized as a response to crisis. It was in this way that we hardly noticed when those digital therapy datasets were sold on for commercial purposes from selling shoes to developing diagnostic tools to 'manage' the big killers of diabetes and obesity (Wired Insider, 2025), digital phenotyping (Torous et al, 2021) and AI psychiatric prescribing. Just a skip and a hop from buying drugs from *Eliza2035*, the next generation of digiceutical prescribing and advertising (Klein, 2023) where our anxieties are contained by conversational AI in the therapeutic call centres of the future (Abd-Alrazaq et al, 2019). This emerging end game of UberTherapy involves the automation of a medical model of mental health that is based on a system of diagnostics. Diagnostic categories are based on available pharmaceuticals and an emerging system of 'theraceuticals' (Hood et al, 2012), introducing the merging of wellbeing and pharmaceuticals by Big Pharma (Simms, 2024). The theraceuticals business model is direct to consumer (D2C) via AI prescriptions and user-pays business models.

There is something strangely reassuring in the narratives of how the robots are going to save us as the wicked problems of care are resolved by innovation and technological solutionism, a welcome alternative to actual care by actual people. If you are an optimist, that the Tech Titans invest $3.7 billion (*Financial Times*, 2021) into digital healthcare, digital companies are sliding into healthcare through acquisition (American Hospital Association, 2023) and ten multinational companies have been invited in to harvest the NHS's data systems (Das et al, 2023) and provide digital services in bulk to the NHS (Tussell, 2022), could make you feel that there is someone powerful looking after us. A mythological universe where benevolent tech leadership and the Cassandras of tech (McShane, 2022) are slugging it out in the sphere of responsible business, offering a compromised ceasefire to the eternal conflict between supply and demand for therapy.

Somewhere around now, the prospect of AI singularity (Vinge, 1993), the technological tipping point when AI overtakes human capacity according to the law of 'accelerating returns' (Kurzweil, 2005), platformization starts to look like a smart move for the psychotherapy professions to move wholesale into the business of e-commerce. As the therapy sector lines up its institutional ducks in the new dawn of private insurance pay-as-you-go digital health, it now seems like a good time to work out if uberization is a pragmatic response to crisis or an industry built on therapeutic unicorns and moodsplaining (Bendell, 2023).

Hi Sigmund™

'Hi, *Hi Sigmund*™ ...There are some things you need to know about me before we start. I don't hate computers or solutions and I genuinely want to be happy. But ...'

Pause for formulation of interpretation. In the clipped tones of a Rhineland immigrant to North London my AI analyst asks about my childhood. My well-rehearsed narrative follows. Of a childhood in rural Britain and isolation. Of being a twin and wearing dressing up to school. Of pet lambs found in the chest freezer. Of being bullied for dancing to The Smiths at a Young Farmers' disco. The metaverse consulting room adapts, powered by text-to-video technology, the couch turns a shade of willow pattern green and the vernacular furniture of my childhood peppers the room. Stories of dark-haired moody boys. An almost imperceptible personalization to *Hi Sigmund*™'s face under the beard to mirror the deliciously delicate bone structure of a middle-aged Timothee Chalamet. Approachability built in through his grey cord three-piece which if you look closely is being held together with staples. A childhood injustice shifting the vocabulary of the interpretation and empathic voice interface[2] to a quiet resignation of Joaquin Phoenix acknowledging the dark underbelly of rural life as survivable and sexy. My life in trade unions, heroes and corporate villains. Nepal. Colombia. Thailand. Tonality and language of political activism creep in to reassure me that my analyst isn't a fascist. My AI analyst's beard grows and omits the synthetic smell of a recent sneaky cigarette. A picture of a mother and son in front of a snowy chalet in the background, offering reassurance that it's OK for me to yearn for solutions to single-parent problems. No jarring mistakes or evasions, no falling asleep during my session unless I request a self-righteous algorithmic invitation to rage. The need to project my deep and ancient anger at another person free in the knowledge that nobody died minus the uncomfortable dynamic of being in a consulting room with someone who is not actually a self-replicated me. The possibility of guiltless ghosting when it feels like something uncomfortable is getting unpacked or the evasion of that we-need-to-talk-about-sex-or-money junction. At night I use wearable neurotechnologies (EPRS, 2023) to data mine my dreams and tap into all that unconscious data which is then fed into the big AI Data Analyst in the sky to design our future therapy on the basis of our collective unconscious. I am contained by the comfort that I don't really have to change, as my past seamlessly predicts my future, same but better.

In *Hi Sigmund*™ I design my own analyst through big data compiled through millions of recorded text and online therapy sessions saved on my personal cloud, my biometric data collected through wearable technologies and my unconscious data analysed through facial emotional recognition technology represented with the use of text-to-video software.[3] The four 'Ps' of the digiceutical business model (Hood et al, 2012) promising a therapy that is exquisitely personalized, designed to predict my needs before I have them, and as such is preventive. A technology that blurs my boundaries in a system of new 'entanglements' (Levy, 2023: 8) in that it surveys my body's data to determine my optimum theraceutical treatment and seamlessly access my private medical insurance account to up my meds to head off my predicted health problems. *Hi Sigmund*™, my AI analyst and pharmaceutical personal shopper.

The session never ends as my AI analyst is infinitely responsive and can text me anytime and anywhere. Where short character interpretations are replaced by chatbot haiku. With no waiting and on-demand I am contained by the reassurance that the present and my future coincide based on millions of clicks and hours of therapeutic labour of the past. A comfort in the appification of my therapy and familiar mobile phone interface which skips lightly over my unconscious data and the daunting possibility of wading through my finely honed defences towards something that actually matters to me. Secure in the trade-off involved in moving from confidentiality to 'pseudoanonymity' (Booth, 2019a), my name and identifying features are removed as a defence against freely associating online. In the name of personalization I am profoundly de-personalized. Much as the idea of *Hi Sigmund*™ seems remote, it is technologically available right now (McKinsey, 2023). Prescription Digital Therapeutics (PDT) which provide software to prescribe treatment, including pharmaceuticals, already exist (Ferrante et al, 2024). Using digital phenotyping to read my biometric data (Pan et al, 2023) even ChatGPT can read my mental patterns to diagnose me (Hadar-Shoval et al, 2023).

As the standardization of therapeutic work into cognitive and behavioural techniques delivered by AI technologies becomes dominant, one of the side effects is that it allows us to indulge in the denial that we have created an unrealistic demand that outweighs realistic supply. As the inherent work intensification involved in the uberization process establishes record levels of burnout and compassion fatigue of human therapists,[4] an AI analyst could genuinely become the preferred option. No more waiting lists, not more careless worn-out actual people. In its current formulation, robot therapy is not a threat to therapy-by-human but in a decade we will see Eliza2035 able to provide a five times a week therapeutic relationship for a fraction of the cost and emerge as a real and recognized socio-cultural object in its own right (Vicari and Kirby, 2023) that challenges what we used to know about therapy.

The interface of smart phones and apps are vehicles for accessing therapy but they are technologies that curate and categorize our experiences (Bowker, 2010). Appification is where data are shaped and shared via a simple download in a way that is not passive in forming our therapeutic experiences. Instead, by design, we are nudged and budged into a version of therapy that is heavily and invisibly curated by algorithms that most of us just do not understand. Appification as the gateway drug for the datafication of healthcare (Pybus and Coté, 2022), and as the AI analyst becomes normalized we will accept them before we understand what they are. Your AI analyst is 'metapolitical' (McQuillan, 2022) in that by introducing apparently neutral technologies into our cultures we redefine quietly and unconsciously what we consider to be politically acceptable and, over time, as UberTherapy comes to dominate the therapeutic space, we will not remember the alternatives.

The therapeutic Wild West

The European Commission's definition of AI 'refers to systems that display intelligent behaviour by analysing their environment and taking actions – with some degree of autonomy – to achieve specific goals' (European Commission, 2018) where data are automatically analysed and patterns identified. Much of what we can call digital therapy is not machine consciousness to any serious degree, instead representing the use of software to carry out analysis and offer specific problem-focused responses. A more advanced form of AI, what Hutter (2012) calls 'universal AI' involves machine learning where behaviour equals or exceeds human competencies – linked to the idea of consciousness but also realistically associated with the capacity to analyse large data sets. Much of what we now call AI is assistive in the sense that it is limited and used to augment our work, rather than generative AI (GenAI) which would allow for fully automated tasks including care work and emotional labour. In one way, this is just a set of technologies available to us but, as you would expect for a book written by a sociologist of work, it takes the hard line that the context within which they are created and used matters obscuring any navigable line between assistive and generative. It is this context that shapes the value, the logics and the intentions of the algorithmic systems that we use. It is also the reason why we would be wise to learn about the trajectory of the therapy sector in the US where uberization happened a decade before the UK, and why this book covers much of the platformization and therapy literature that comes from the US.

In another way, UberTherapy is just trickle-down monopoly capitalism (Weigel, 2023). A familiar landscape of free trade/deregulation, the emergence of multinational corporations (MNCs) and a constantly emerging 'global shift' (Dicken, 2015) in the scope of supply chains capitalizing on weak regulation and the invitation to outsource employers' responsibilities. Under this system, international financial and European banking systems (Cooiman, 2023) opened the doors to venture capital and introduced a short-term, profit-driven logic into mental health care. As the model of care became corporatized and commodified, we saw the consequences of turning patients into consumers, where the rules of the market determine what care exists and who gets it, laying the foundations of a healthcare model based on what we could call neoliberal paternalism (Sanford and Silverman, 2012). Neoliberal paternalism in the UK is a distinctly British story about the NHS and successive government attempts to wind down systems of welfare and care. I call this the 'Cheer up love' mental health policy adopted in the UK somewhere around 2008 (see Chapter 3) as austerity came to define what constituted a mental health service. It is this unwavering belief in austerity that set the trajectory for the sharp rise in UK Employee Assistance Programmes (EAPs) and online therapy platforms precisely to normalize private medical insurance and allow the state to walk away from universal healthcare towards a system of psychic pilates where you can get what you need if you can pay for it.

Some of the UberTherapy story is about the industrialization of care (see Chapter 3) and about how public mental health services were so transformed into a system of therapy 'lite' as an increasingly automated system of analysis as an alternative to deep relational work. Government policy aligned itself to the emergence of private medical insurance built on a digital model of 'personalized' care designed for data capture and personalized assessments (CDEI, 2019) that in reality depersonalize by offering short-term, solution-focused CBT-Lite to everyone. A cheap and politically convenient model of therapy in that it defines the problem at the level of individual cognitions and behaviours (Dalal, 2018) placing the responsibility to recover with the individuals involved rather than the systems (Mills, 2014) within which they exist. Once this industrialization took place, the scene was set for its deindustrialization through digitalization, platformization and automation of therapeutic work. The platformization that we are now seeing across the therapy sector involves different and often interlocked characteristics. Crowdsourcing which we can define as 'internet-enabled labour exchange' (Barnes et al, 2015) and the sharing economy came into play, characterized by online peer-to-peer exchange of services and assets as part of the gig economy, characterized as precarious and temporary which ticks the boxes of the financial and digital logics of platformization (Liang et al, 2022).

The story of UberTherapy is AngloAmerican where, if we look West, we can see the future of therapy writ large. Angerland is a litigious corporate system where Accepted Standards of Care and parity of esteem is slogged out in court – big legal cases that stand as an extraordinary disincentive to professional and policy actors in challenging the model of UberTherapy (Bendat, 2023).

In the US we have seen the escalation of text-based 'therapy' platforms operating state-wide services for teenagers where teens experiencing distress can message a therapist any time through an app plus one 30-minute virtual session each month. Therapy for all, no need to wait, on demand 24/7, actual words and emojis. The UberTherapy that is being offered here has a compelling business case. No more waiting lists, no more diagnosis or complex co-morbidity, just consumers and entrepreneurs (Ticona and Mateescu, 2018). Except when you remember that these therapy consumers include children and young people, and that these same providers have a robust history of legal action taken by the Federal Trade Commission (FTC) in relation to repeated consumer data breaches. It seems like an enormous gamble to take on our mental states to place ourselves within this, something which makes sense when you know that one of the 'side effects' of some psychiatric medication can be an increased propensity to gambling addiction (MHRA, 2023) and the link between digital therapy platforms and the gambling sector (Davies, 2020).

In the UK we have already had trade deal discussions between the US and UK precisely to access NHS data and its data-management systems in the face of corporate bankruptcies (McKiernan, 2024), lack of supply chain monitoring and patient data breaches (Booth, 2019a). Far from this being a few bad corporate eggs, this is now how it works in the NHS. By blurring the lines of who owns what – who owns the data, who owns the intellectual property that it holds, who gets to use it to develop more apps and digital products that then get sold back to the NHS – it stops us naming names and disarms us from seeing the end game of UberTherapy.

To understand the UberTherapy endgame requires us to dig deeper into the AngloAmerican story of healthcare. Anne Case and Angus Deaton's *Deaths of Despair* (2020) maps the remarkable story of the US private healthcare system's 'upward redistribution' of money to investors through its promise of attrition and a two-tier system that only responds to the needs of the people paying insurance. This model is under-articulated in the digital therapy debates, but the institutional ducks are lining up to link private medical insurance, EAPs and on-demand direct to consumer access to iCBT-Lite delivered by a chatbot, AI mental health diagnostics (wearable technologies still optional) plus automated prescribing powers. As we know from the US, the prices of pharmaceuticals and digital technologies are three times higher than they are currently in the UK (Case and Deaton, 2020) which is a red flag that the emerging model of private medical insurance and pay-as-you-go treatment in the UK is based on a theraceutical business model.

Whatever political party is in power in the UK, the digital and scalable model of theraceutical consumption, of direct to consumer personalized pricing and platform subscriptions and prescriptions based on biometric data from birth (Simms, 2024) is going to happen. It is in the circularity of the new business of mental health that, at its most stark, sets the trajectory of recovery back towards taking drugs. If you think that this is unconscious you should know that the two central anxiety and depression questionnaires used in the NHS (GAD-7 and PHQ-9) were developed, researched and sponsored by one of the largest pharmaceutical companies in the world, which might raise a question about how it came to be that 80 per cent of the people who take the tests are prescribed antidepressants (Davis, 2021).

Not wishing to over-state the heroic nature of thinking critically, it is important to understand the risks of challenging online therapy platforms out loud, particularly on social media and particularly if you have some reach within the therapy sector. Although UberTherapy's legal teams have turned their litigious attention to the enshrinement of emerging international and national platform work regulation into national law and the years of legal precedence that will now follow, it is still possible that UberTherapy might sue you. It might even consider suing you for asking a simple question like whether this is real therapy (see Chapter 6). If you feel that is unlikely, the most useful book you could read is about the fight for deep therapy in the US, *Advancing Psychotherapy for the Next Generation* (Michaels et al, 2023) which should give you a roadmap to surviving the future therapy sector.

Since we appear to have entered the therapeutic Wild West, this seems like a good time to ask how bad can it get under platform capitalism and a pay-as-you-go on-demand private medical insurance healthcare system underpinned by venture capital?

Size matters

Academics do not agree on a definition of platformization (Liang et al, 2022) nor do they agree on the extent of augmentation, automation or threat to decent work that are implied by AI technologies. That is as it should be because the business model shifts as consumer and labour force characteristics change and as monopoly capitalism moves its focus onto what can make money right now. Part of the problem is understanding that UberTherapy is a profound change brought about by platformization not just in how therapy is done but in its extractive value (McCroskey, 2024). UberTherapy shifts the focus away from therapy towards an extraction industry – the de-industrial extraction of data and the therapeutic labour. Layered on top of this is its policy ROI of getting people into work and off benefits, something that is financially compelling at least in the short term, particularly if you do not collect the data on the attrition this involves (see Chapters 2 and 3).

I am grateful to Dana Mattioli for writing *The Everything War* (Mattioli, 2024) not least because it arrived literally two weeks before I had to submit the first manuscript for UberTherapy, just in time to give me a much needed injection of clarity about what is at stake with UberTherapy. The book outlines Amazon's business model, and how it came to be that, in one way or another, even when we are having therapy we are engaged in a new world of e-commerce. They map the attempts by the FTC in the US to use antitrust laws to place limits on attempts by Amazon to take over the commercial world, highlighting the long-term research and work of the FTC Chair, Lina Khan, to articulate the paradox inherent in a model where only size matters. In the 2023 FTC lawsuit against Amazon, the charge was that it maintains its illegal monopoly precisely to raise prices across its e-commercial platform. It did this using an algorithm codenamed Project Nessie to test raise its own brand prices, watching its competitors do the same, and then dropping the prices once profits had been secured. As an investigative journalist, Dana had worked out that during 2016–2018 Project Nessie secured US$1bn in additional profits from raising its own and its competitors' prices.

Another last-minute arrival was Ben Shestakofsky's *Behind the Startup* (2024) which is a good roadmap of the growth of venture capital behind US digital start-ups in the 2020s, and using their own privilege (of being white, young and male and therefore blending in to the digital start-up landscape) to write a good book. Their book joins some important dots about UberTherapy by pointing out that half of the global total of venture capital is from the US, at $311bn in 2021. It clarifies that the end game for venture capital is corporate acquisitions or Initial Public Stock Offerings (IPOs) as a way of liquidizing inflated assets. The financial logic of venture capital is therefore fundamentally rooted in inflating its value by gaming its economic performance in order to allow equity to exit with massive profits.

If we follow this logic, the platformization of therapy represents a seismic shift in its future trajectory when UberTherapy's business model is to take up the therapy space as a platform for health e-commerce in the attention market. Five of the 12 therapists advertised on the therapy platforms will offer CBT-Lite, text-based services will be delivered through integrated platforms in your home via built-in devices. Therapists will become just the people behind the platforms, the click workers surviving on predatory prices and wage theft (see Chapter 4). You will pay a dynamic price, unsustainably low, but seduced by the offer of avoiding a day spent haggling with your insurance company if you can live with the guilty secret that your affordable therapy is likely to pay your therapist below minimum wage. This demand for continuous growth in the platform economy will, in turn, influence the nature of the therapeutic relationship where patients become 'Homo consumens' (Fromm, 1976: 153) demanding a restless and insecure and ultimately 'indifferent' on-demand consumption of therapy that offers a flight from the facts of life.

With UberTherapy's failure to make profits in its annual returns, and the compensation cases for non-delivery of therapeutic unicorns and shareholder class action compensation (Larson, 2024) for overstating its worth, or cashing in its IPO, it might feel like its positivity bubble is about to burst (Lanxon, 2019). With McKinseyed claims of the economic potential of generative AI to add US$2.6 trillion to the global economy (McKinsey, 2023), it is easy to think UberTherapy is just a Silicon Valley bubble. From the bankruptcy of digital health data companies to the US listed companies operating in the UK's primary care sector (Simister, 2023), we might seek comfort in believing this to be the next tech bubble. But as the Tech Titans unlock their shares and record valuations (Hodgson, 2024) and we are spammed with adverts for online therapy platforms, we do not actually know if we are watching the crash and burn of the therapy rollercoaster, or just swinging at the top of a broken Ferris wheel wondering where it will all end in Angerland.

The datafication of despair

In Nick Srnicek's important book *Platform Capitalism* (2017) they explain that platformization reorientates our economies to data-driven growth. Platformization is fundamentally based on datafication which monetizes and therefore values data such that whatever the nature of that work is, from cab rides to therapy, it is done to produce data, sell those data, and increase value either to develop further AI products, or for commercial use, or to raise the share price before the final buyout or listing. Platforms offer new ways to create value beyond economies of scale and price through extracting data which they can then sell as intermediaries to other sectors and platforms (Rahman and Thelen, 2019). The business model is not just about cutting costs and standardizing products, it also incorporates the capacity to control supply chains and markets through the size of its networks (Rahman and Thelen, 2019). As such, uberization involves a 'deindustrialization' where what we produce – goods or services or therapy – becomes immaterial as long as it can be commodified into the right kind of data that can then generate value. This then leads to the use of technological intermediaries and standardized data extraction tools to mine the data from, in the case of UberTherapy, the therapeutic labour of the therapist and the consumer. In order to sell or analyse those data to develop further digital assets and AI technologies. That can be sold on. Round and round, up and down we go on the therapy rollercoasters.

One of the consistent characteristics of researching health data and platformization is that despite the growing data privacy campaigns[5] most people are not scared enough to care much if they lose their data. As people used to say in unions, 'I don't mind if they tap my phone, I've done nothing wrong', but a growing paranoia thanks to the data hacking of therapeutic information and blackmail cases in the egalitarian haven of Nordic social democracy (Ralston, 2021) we are all starting to realize that where a model of pseudoanonymity replaces confidentiality there can be profound consequences for the consumers of UberTherapy. Our anxieties about our AI-MHS should grow when we know that data breaches by therapy apps include a text-based suicide hotline (Levine, 2022) and emotional support apps for kids (Ruiz, 2024).

Part of the rationale for gamification is the datafication of healthcare where the data that are captured – financial, biometric, personal – can be sold on to other companies. The big data that can be sold to LLMs to churn out more data and the evidence base for new AI technologies is routinely collected both from text and recorded online sessions. I have not put a link there because this section is not intended to launch any law suits, rather to just state a fact about reality that personal therapy data are being collected one way or another by online therapy platforms and have been in the NHS for at least a decade. Other consumer data can be sold on to digital marketing companies to switch on personalized marketing and includes not just platforms but more traditional charities and third sector organizations (Das, 2023).

AI technologies are predictive systems in that they predict what is needed on the basis of past data and, as such, they are vulnerable to eugenic outcomes (Buolamwini, 2023). Even in the automated work of therapy chatbots, there is no explanation or contextualization just industrialized measurements of our states of mind in order to allow for commodity exchange. The problem with disembodied data like these is that they support and promote bias and with it pre-existing inequalities deepen. In Chun's remarkable writing (Chun, 2021), they cut through the technical and go straight to the political with a confidence that is extremely useful for those of us who have never designed an algorithm. They summarize the design processes that lead algorithms to discriminate centred around the use of the discriminatory data of the past to evidence discriminatory predictions into the future. Because of the use of past data and their inherited bias, the data infrastructure itself can be underpinned by eugenic assumptions. Rather than acting as a benign mechanism for sharing they also do this invisibly so that we can and do ignore any discrimination that follows, which in turn amplifies it. This is why the calling out by the Cassandras of tech including Joy Buolamwini's Algorithmic Justice League (Buolamwini, 2023) and Timnit Gebru's public engagement over facial recognition technology, are so crucial in throwing a spanner into the algorithmic circle of hell we are now in.

It is in this sense that UberTherapy is an extractive industry and one which performs a 'data colonialism', that hollows out the social and creates new social knowledge that is based on 'commercial targeting' (Couldry and Mejias, 2019: 128). We are being measured and 'socially quantified' (Couldry and Mejias, 2019: 129) in order for us to consume more. Wearing our biometric technologies on the promise of personalization we become strangely depersonalized by the proxies that are set to categorize us and predict what we need/will consume rather than whether we are recovering.

Much of the data mining that is happening now is unseen by consumers in part because of the use of APIs and the seamless exchange-without-permission between software and websites that we inevitably engage with online. Platforms and their hybrid siblings use, to varying degrees, certain design features including application programming interfaces (APIs) and software development kits (SDKs) that allow data and information to be communicated between websites and apps in order to organize and promote value-creating activities. Whatever your reasons for signing up for UberTherapy, the system is designed to extract what it needs from you and not the other way around.

As the selling off of COVID-19 data and the fast tracking of health ambitions of the logistics Tech Titans expose, this is not about health; it is about market control (King, 2022). This is why every time you see a friendly trusted doctor's face on your screen you should squint to see the black and green algorithm raining down behind them to understand what is being exchanged between you. What is valued here is not your health but the smooth transition from data (what is given) to capta (what is taken) (Loukissas, 2019) as the currency for digital therapy (Murgia, 2022). It is this financial logic that needs to be kept in mind as the moderate digital health voices call for app regulation (D. Cox, 2024) while the funding for research projects to measure the degrees of app efficacy continues. None of which addresses the financial imperative of UberTherapy that relies on the extraction of our psychic data and is willing to pay the FTC's US$m dollar fines for routine data breaches this requires.

Sabor a Mierda

Five minutes into *Matrix Resurrections*, in among the dark urban landscape there is a neon sign on the rooftop of a rent by the hour hotel flashing '*Sabor a Mierda*', subject to much debate on Reddit and signalling the sick-gut-feeling that everything in the Matrix is not what it seems. In business school handbooks it is standard to see module reading lists include film and documentaries as a way of digesting the speed at which platformization and digitalization are taking place. In the matrix, the use of cultural references in higher education would be reframed as Micky Mouse degrees crushing hopes of graduate employability (Haynes, 2024) with academics lazily rolling out videos instead of actual teaching about the health- and work-related benefits in our digital future. I do not think that speaking our truth in the confessional spaces of social media is the same thing as speaking truthfully, but one of the arguments throughout this book is to call on us to use our senses to re-embody the debates about what is happening to therapy as a result of its digitalization. To accept that our psychic realities and the way we experience them in our bodies gives us important information of another order allows us to use this intangible sense of *sabor a mierda* to navigate the new business of mental health.

In the field of big data there is a phrase that says if you put shit in you get shit out. Bad data are mined, and used to develop AI technologies which are based on a shaky evidence-based ground. Part of this is about the gamification of recovery performance data such that therapy can become performative on both sides. There is also a lingering *sabor a mierda* in the way we measure recovery and the way we do not measure those clients who fall through the systems of attrition by design, intentionally caught up in a call centre cul-de-sac and signposted out of services.

As we explore in Chapter 3, when CBT-Lite claims 50 per cent recovery, extending to 75 per cent for iCBT-Lite, we know that we are playing a game of attrition where anyone living with distress to any severity or complexity cannot easily be genuinely helped using this model of therapy. UberTherapy is a system that measures an inflated sense of its own success and ignores its clinical failures by making clients fill in standardized questionnaires at the end of every session until they indicate sufficient improved mood to be taken off the books. Picture this, the face of your 24-year-old psychology graduate beaming hopefully at you asking if you feel better after each session? When the smoke and mirrors of self-reporting questionnaires replaces the holy grail of clinical diagnosis and your first 'treatment' is by someone working in a call centre with no diagnostic training, you have to ask the question what exactly are consumers of digital therapy recovering from?

Within the platform business model is an idea of 'enshittification' (Doctorow, 2023) to describe the trajectory of the UberTherapy business model which survives on providing subsidized commodities until the point that users, subscribers and personal data are pooled, profits are reported and shares may be sold and then the company folds. On some level we know this and feel it in our guts which should alert us to the nature of the socio-economic project under way. It is a hall of mirrors where nothing is as it seems until you close your eyes and re-engage with the what-it-feels-like.

In psychoanalytic thinking there is a lot of time spent looking at defences against anxiety – where we project or split the feelings we cannot accept into others. In therapy there is an invitation to explore our attempts to 'dump-and-run' and think about those projections with a therapist in order to do the work of therapy. For many therapists, receiving and working through the projections of their clients is the raw material for doing some good work. I might be pushing the shit leitmotif too far here, but there is an idea in psychotherapy about a toilet therapist that might be helpful in understanding the inevitability of the attack that is taking place on UberTherapists in this Bad-Therapy-Bad-Therapists narrative. In Abigail Shrier's book *Bad Therapy* (Shrier, 2024), looking at child and adolescent therapy in the US and the ideological issues at play, they explain the rise of bad therapy by going for the individualist jugular. Using their journalistic skills to formulate a narrative about the attack on parenting that is taking place, and to record what happens when therapy goes wrong, they explain this as a consequence of the practices of bad therapists. I am not saying that there are not therapeutic harms or bad therapists, there are and it is important that bad practice is called out, talked about and subject to the scrutiny of the professional regulators in a way they can be learned from. But there is something too compelling in its simple explanatory line about the failures of digital therapy caused by individual therapists rather than the business model they are working within.

In psychoanalytic thinking, anxiety and our defences against it are given central place, particularly our common attempts to split off and project our anxiety externally. In this model, the threat of our aggression killing off something we love, like a decent therapist, triggers a projection of the parts of ourselves we cannot accept – our 'shit' – into the toilet therapist to rid ourselves of these 'shitty' feelings. I agree, probably too much about shit, but given that we are talking about therapy that acknowledges our infant experiences of love and hate, extractions and evictions, of the 'toilet-breast' (Meltzer, 1967) and the retreat into blaming mummy for everything, it is not entirely out of context. I want to raise it as a possibility that the blaming of the individual UberTherapist for the failings of a business model of therapy has deeper causes.

One of the problems with therapy is that just saying what is on your mind means breaking through our personal and societal defences, and it is in this ordinary way that therapy that draws on relational and psychoanalytic theory is, in the right hands, radical (Layton, 2020). The work of therapy involves not just us breaking down our defences, but also being critical of cultural and political and economic norms that set the fault lines of what can be said and not said out loud. It is in the forensic detective work of therapy that the critical linking work also gets done – the breaking down and piecing together of our lives that is in stark contrast to the disassociated cultures of social media and appification.

The really shaming part of the rating and ranking of your UberTherapist is that it is so easily and unconsciously done in the platformed therapy sector, with a simple click of a consumer satisfaction survey. In addition to the consequences for the UberTherapist's employability, the hit is also felt by the consumers of online therapy platforms. Since we are talking about therapy rather than a food delivery, the hit is not in the abstract, because the violation of algorithmic transgression is always embodied. Whether online or face to face in the consulting room, the attempt to project something we do not want into the therapist always has a consequence for us; one which we experience in our bodies, whether conscious or not. Allowing us to retreat back into finely honed defences to avoid saying what is really on our minds, for many of us trashing the hard therapeutic work required to do just that simple thing. It means that whatever shame inhabits us, heightened for those of us who have experienced trauma, can trigger anxiety and its associated defences, shutting down the parts of ourselves that are most likely to protect us; the parts of us that are most likely to relate. That is, the ordinary human parts of ourselves that are not being busy-busy rating and ghosting each other as a defence in an algorithmic system that allows us to easily override a key fact of life – that we need each other to heal and to grow.

Defences against thinking

One of the themes of this book is that UberTherapy mis-sells the product because it is a business model directed towards selling drugs on TikTok, not therapy. Through advertising, UberTherapy plays on our insecurities and offers a D2C solution for that, marketed on the attention economy; as we go up and down the platform rollercoasters feeling like losers, we will buy more stuff.

Psychoanalytic theory is full of literature that tries to understand the attack on thinking that can take place within therapy. Being challenged by questions of anger, money and sex can ordinarily trigger the dynamic process of denial and projection in us, and this is core material for the process of working through that therapy offers its consumers whether on- or offline. This is important for us to understand: that part of what happens in the growth of on-demand therapy is the attack on our thinking about it. It is by not thinking about the risks of on-demand therapy and nudging each other into a 'could-be-worse' defence that we become complicit in us reaching the logical conclusion of platformization, which is that it becomes a sub-division in the sector of e-commerce.

If you can stand to use the language of ethical leadership there is something useful in the act of understanding our complicity in the systems we engage with. Max Bazerman (2023) argues that while we cannot regulate around the intention to do harm, we can do a lot to set regulatory parameters around organizational and financial models by not relying on the 'la-la-la-I-can't-hear-you' survival strategy that some of us in the therapy sector have relied on. That we now have private equity providing sexual assault support systems, and nameless international investment holding sensitive public data, should worry us much more than it does (Marsh and Garcia, 2024). How this happened was by us not asking the right questions in our standardized self-reported questionnaires or not challenging the new business of mental health by not talking about it. This means that we are at a crucial point in the defence of therapy while there is still a memory of the principles and practices of therapy, and it is in this way that we stand at the tipping point in the 'race to the bottom' that UberTherapy potentially represents.

It is true to say that not everyone is designed to stare into the abyss, but one of the problems with living in Angerland is that it plays upon our ambivalence of having relationships with other people. During the pandemic and enforced lockdown, many of us were fine about not being with other people and many of us felt good about not having to go to work. Life is often about what the alternatives are, and if the offer is a burned out NHS therapist after a 12-month waiting list for guided self-help and endless mood questionnaires, it is legitimate to ask if a digital something is better than the emerging clinical nothing. But what AI systems cannot do, by design, is to contextualize, to think critically and to resolve conflicts (Marshall, 2022); a profound political deficit in the emerging interlock between authoritarian systems and AI technologies, and an unsafe environment for therapeutic work.

One of the proposals explored in this book is the idea that digital therapy offers us a defence against thinking about the facts of life. Throughout the writing of this book I have read and re-read Robert Money-Kyrle's 1960s' papers about a psychoanalytic framing of the political self (see Money-Kyrle, 1961), partly because of the nuance in among the big strokes of his writing, and partly because it was one of the first writings that made it possible for me to respect my political mind while having analysis. There are three different but interlinked facts of life presented in *Man's Picture of His World* (Money-Kyrle, 1961) and throughout this book I try to formulate them in relation to the AI world that we are now living in. The proposal is that digital therapy and the use of an AI analyst can be seen as a defence against the three intertwined facts of life, unavoidably writ large in therapeutic processes and for anyone who needs to do the internal work of repair. First that we are dependent on others to grow – not to be 'connected' or to swipe left, but to allow ourselves to need others and to navigate that. Second that we are not self-replicating and come into being through a creative act that we are excluded from, and this requires that our aspirations to be the biggest and the best are kept in their place. Then we die – the third fact is that time is not infinite and all things end beyond our control, despite the seduction of being able to relate on-demand and ghost people before they leave us.

I now believe that the platformization of therapy offers an intentional unknowing about our psychic realities. It allows for the normalizing of UberTherapy that is designed to deny relational care and hide the data and algorithmic evidence that stops us knowing the facts and taking a position on them. It is a neoliberal framework that does not offer us a stable 'framework of care' (Weintrobe, 2021) where we are safe to work out who we really are. This algorithmic unknowing also applies to UberTherapists, where the denial of class and money in the therapy profession serves to evade the political work of challenging the systemic degradation of people-who-need-to-earn, while maintaining the decreasing circles of professional privilege. The part of the therapy profession that, ironically, chooses not to raise its own consciousness or, in the language of Freire (1970), to confront our internal oppressors, who say that this degraded model of therapeutic labour is all we deserve leaving us unable to talk about UberTherapy, something you almost could not make up.

Part of the competitive advantage of digital therapy is that it underemphasizes the unconscious in the consulting room. Hanna Zeavin's book *The Distance Cure* (2021) was the first book, and the first academic, to offer me some encouragement that the idea of UberTherapy had legs. In a meticulous record of the past and present of teletherapy they introduce the idea of 'auto-intimacy' (Zeavin, 2021) promoted through auto-therapy. It is here in this paradoxical idea of automated intimacy where the vocabulary of therapy is delinked from bodily and psychic realities, creating a buffer to the frustrations of being human and the psychic reality that all things about us have a complex history. By using techniques or frameworks designed to draw on what is only consciously said, digital therapy offers us a way to evade the central psychic fact that it is other people who see our unconscious, not us. It is through the communication and listening, observing and dreams shared between two or more people that we come to know the unconscious parts of ourselves we are designed to bury. My therapist can see things I cannot about myself. No more fantasies of a manicured me, or wasting sessions pedicuring Hair-n-Teeth's hooves to deny the fundamental insecurity of needing others who are inevitably unreliable, who do not mirror us, and who die.

The Tinderesque sleight of hand of UberTherapy redefines the intimacy problem as one of meeting people rather than relating to them. An interface where the breathtaking speed of endings are built in through the iconic design functionality of wading through infinite relational possibilities through rapid, repeated, binary and visually focused swipe movements. It is in this way that the design premise of UberTherapy redefines the therapy problem as one of convenience and choice where if it can be done anytime from anywhere by anyone then the problem of relating has been solved. The problem with UberTherapy is that whenever you are dealing with actual people you are dealing with the what we do not want to say and its unconscious communication. Far from increasing the accuracy of cues followed by interpretations, the risk is that the standardized and digitalized model of care does not capture us as we actually are, and predictive technologies can never know about our future growth and adaptation. For many of us who come from a place of early trauma the denial of the chance for change and growth is a big problem when the ways in which we seek help can repeat the emotional and developmental neglect of our past. With the emergence of short-term, solution-focused and ultimately 'nonrelational therapies' (Philipson, 1993: 155), we are left with a set of transactional decisions about what kind of therapy to buy online.

As you would expect for a psychoanalytically informed book written by a trade unionist, I do not believe that for the key players in the business model of UberTherapy this is unconscious. Instead, I argue that it is an attempt to silence people by disorienting and distracting us from the reality that the chain of responsibility of UberTherapy is unintelligible. In these algorithmic systems of work we are all set up for failure to mis-sell the product and then blame ourselves for its failure to deliver recovery, a cruelty to the next generation of therapists and their customers who have no living memory of what the alternatives are. It keeps us spinning round and round on the therapy rollercoasters, unable to think straight about what is really happening to us. It is still possible that UberTherapy is not our only future because when the rollercoasters of venture capital crash and burn, we will still be us lugging around our anger and shame and there will still be good therapists wanting to work with that.

The ultimate litmus test for *RealTherapy*™ used in this book is that whatever therapeutic tradition or technology we engage in, it has to help us acknowledge and navigate these facts of life rather than hinder us by offering a retreat into self-sufficiency and a technological defensiveness. In Angerland, we are invited to accept the 'pathological side-effect' (Rustin, 2013: 183) of AI technologies which allow us to deny the fundamentally collective nature of getting our needs met. In turn, our failed attempts at dependency-via-platform are used as ammunition to further denigrate the act of relating where our customer dissatisfaction nudges us into survivalist thinking premised on other people being dangerous.

The sheer scale of Angerland that is emerging obscures responsibility and intentionally underestimates the significance of our agency. As the mainstream institutions and research around the efficacy of mental health apps grinds on in its industrial intention to keep the Angerland show on the road, even the emerging responsible business lobby runs the risk of working only in the shallows and being co-opted by UberTherapy. All the while we are going round and round the platform rollercoasters, distracting us from the important critical thinking we have to do to know if we can change the logic of the algorithm away from a financial to a therapeutic one. In Angerland, it is not the hope that kills you it is the naked indifference of the delinquent teenagers running the rides and their venture capitalist gangmasters you have to watch.

Notes

[1] Rorschach Test, www.rorschach.org/
[2] Empathic Voice Interface, www.hume.ai/products#empathicVoiceInterface
[3] Open AI, Sora, https://openai.com/sora
[4] The Future of Therapy, www.thefutureoftherapy.org
[5] Mozilla Foundation, Privacy Not Included campaign, https://foundation.mozilla.org/en/privacynotincluded/

2

UberTherapy

The architecture of UberTherapy

This chapter lays out the UberTherapy architecture – the range of business models and technologies that make up the structures of platformization and the logics that underpin them. There are no agreed definitions of what platforms are as they are made up of interrelated processes and fluid business models. Platforms can be understood as 'institutional chameleons' (Vallas and Schor, 2020) that provide an online interface that digitally coordinates interactions between sellers of things or services and consumers. Some provide services that are geographically located, others provide 'cloudwork' from anywhere in the world (Huws et al, 2019), some provide business to business (B2B) services, others business to consumer (B2C), increasingly selling direct to consumer (D2C) and some are hybrid.

The process of platformization in therapy is part of a broader process of uberization involving two shifts in the logic and the labour processes of therapy towards industrialization (marketization and standardization of therapy through a model of CBT-Lite) and then, counterintuitively, deindustrialization (a data-driven model of profit and growth and use of AI technologies through a model of iCBT-lite). Uberization has, in fact, been around for a long time as much of it involves outsourcing and subcontracting, just digitally facilitated via crowdsourcing. A kind of AI outsourcing but still reliant on the work of millions of us, some of which (number still unknown) are therapists. This is not to deny that there is something specific going on with UberTherapy but it is to suggest that the way that AI is being used deepens outsourcing trends that we have seen for decades (Vertesi, 2024). It is a model that allows companies to outsource employers' responsibilities and having to employ skilled and technical staff to do the work. It allows for massively higher numbers of people becoming available for work, the vast majority of whom will be precarious in this highly racialized and feminized on-demand workforce aligned to the phenomenon of temporary agency work (van Doorn, 2017). Some theorists see platforms as 'meta-organizations' where there is a structured relationship with sellers or 'complementors', while others use the language of 'entrepreneurs' operating in the share economy (Chen et al, 2022). Some online platforms have advanced forms of algorithmic management through digital design features, backed up with consumer rating mechanisms and associated sanctions for poor performance.

This chapter explores the range of characteristics of UberTherapy and to make this understandable I use a typology of different models of UberTherapy to explore these different processes that can exist within online platforms.

- *Digitalization (DigitalBFF)*: Partly due to the pandemic, therapy was rapidly digitalized via routine use of teletherapy and online guided self-help, and with it the rise in text-based services accessed through smart phones and digital devices.
- *Platformization B2C (TotalRecovery)*: Online platforms work as intermediaries between individual clients and providers (B2C). This often involves online platforms with algorithmic management.
- *Platformization B2B (RemotelyHelpful)*: Online platforms offering therapy as intermediaries between clients and providers (B2B), including EAPs. These can involve outsourcing or direct employment of therapists either involving algorithmic management using a platform or not.
- *Appification (Eliza2035)*: This involves the use of apps to access services predominantly through mobile phones, including conversational AI, chatbots, tracking and auditing technologies and text-based services.
- *Datafication (Minotaur)*: The collection and analysis of data sets, including recorded sessions, to be sold for use in e-commerce or used to develop AI technologies.

It's always all about sex

As part of the research for this book I accessed as many apps and online therapy platforms as I could tolerate. I would periodically dip into apps that provided text-based contact, guided self-help and chatbots, including official NHS and commercial ones, some free, some I paid for. Although this, for me, is not therapy, I wanted to test this as a gateway drug, and whether it would direct me back into other UberTherapy offers. As a trade unionist who worked in Eastern Europe in the 1990s, I learned never to switch on my GPS and exercise a thin layer of paranoia in all outward-facing digital activity, explaining why I do not write that many formal emails and never crack open a chatroom to say what I really think. While researching this book I acquired a separate phone and computer and adopted my porn name.

I treated this part of the research as a form of self-harm rationed to a few hours a week while I wrote a journal and tucked away my memory of actual therapy in a mental box. I also had lots of in-person therapy and discussed research ethics at length with colleagues and researcher friends. When I had set my risk management research parameters I let Hair-n-Teeth out of its cave. I used this damaged part of me because given that many people seeking help will come from trauma, we may as well test the system against our needs (Kuzminskaite et al, 2022). It means that the information of another order that is gathered here provides a parallel universe of experience distinct from the consumer reviews and self-reporting questionnaires documenting the stellar progress of a clientele who can make immediate use of on-demand therapy because they can formulate what they want to achieve and why. My research focused on the things that for most of us are the hardest to talk about in therapy – anger, money and sex – to test the depth of the work that can be done online.

RemotelyHelpful

RemotelyHelpful provide EAPs mainly in the public sector including higher education, where they are establishing student assistance programmes (SAPs) on the same short-term CBT model. I called them as my then employer had a contract with them. This was my first experience of an online therapy platform.

First contact was with a young call centre worker – I explained that I was being bullied at work and that I was feeling overwhelmed. That I was a single parent to a pre-school child, moved to a rural area during lockdown, with old parents one of whom was in hospital and that I had a 2.5-hour commute each way to work. I said that I needed to talk to someone urgently as I was worried I was about to have a nervous breakdown. In response to the question about suicide I dramatically cheered up and almost shouted 'I'm fine'. Young person said someone would call me back at an unspecified time in the future.

Waited two weeks. Subsequent calls to call centre met with low level hysteria by the unknown people who answered – we're really busy, you're low down on the food chain because you're not suicidal. I offered my sympathy and shouted 'I'm fine' in a way that you don't need to be Freud to know was a barefaced lie.

Three weeks later I received a phone message while I was teaching from a therapist whose name I couldn't hear asking me to call back. Four call centre contact calls later I was given the name of the person who called me and told they would call me back. Each time I called I had to repeat my story, increasingly in short hand, increasingly feeling unsafe even though I was always conscious that this was, for me, a research exercise. Kicking myself for using some actual facts about myself. Managed to ask what I could at best expect from *RemotelyHelpful* and a young person who was in breach of their associate mental health practitioner contract went to find out that I would be allowed six sessions of CBT. I laughed way too loudly.

Therapist calls again while I'm teaching. Leaves message. Three months after the initial contact I call again to speak to a woman who apologizes and says that I have been taken off the list of people seeking support because I didn't answer two phone calls. You know, the ones that happened while I was teaching. Because this is an EAP dominant in the education sector right so I guess you understand that I am a teacher. Call handler was a sympathetic older woman. In the time we were waiting for the computer to unfreeze they told me how bad their daughter's university is and how they weren't surprised I was being bullied. I don't think they actually described my life as a 'shit show' but I felt genuine human pity coming down the phone which wasn't helpful. They said they'd do their best for me when I asked rather snippily that I wasn't matched with a 24-year-old psychology graduate. They said they understood perfectly and typed 'old' on my digital notes.

A week later I spoke to the therapist I was matched to. Their video camera didn't work so they saw me and I didn't see her. I didn't want to get over-complex about the power dynamics of that but it felt like a job interview. We did another assessment this time using a standardized questionnaire. They apologized, said it was required, problems with it but better than the alternative. We did an additional assessment which was more humane in that I could say what I wanted, and then asked me if I had any questions. I didn't honestly have the heart to ask anything personal so I switched back to researcher mode and I ask if this is confidential and if the sessions are in any way recorded. I asked because unless someone checks my name against my employer how do they know I am covered by *RemotelyHelpful*? They said they'd never been asked that question and will let me know in the next session.

Next session happens the following week. Again no camera. They report that the sessions are not recorded. I ask if we is using a *RemotelyHelpful* platform, they say no too quickly for me to have a sense of whether they know that or want to believe it. Having talked through with my own therapist the ethics of going on with this process I had already decided to end the sessions but to avoid my therapist not getting paid and to allow them to record our contact as 'successful' treatment I attended a second session. They agree that my life is actually awful (their words not mine) and six sessions won't touch the sides. It's you not me. Offers to give me private therapy since we seem to get on really well. Said they could see why they matched us. Felt like a bad date.

During this period something unexpected happened at work and very rapidly using my workplace EAP started to feel dangerous. Tapping into my real experiences of PTSD related to previous workplace bullying and years of being gaslit into 'managing' my feelings. And even though on one level I understood the game that was being played, my body reacted in exactly the same way as it does in the face of threat. The cortisol pumped through my body and I heard the swish swash of my hypertension. Night sweats followed as Hair-n-Teeth was dragged out of its cave and I was left with feelings of deep shame for thinking I could step outside of my own nervous system for the sake of researching a book. I felt angry and dirty for touching something I knew was dangerously sub-therapeutic for someone like me.

TotalRecovery

This is one of the most promoted B2C online therapy platforms in the UK. For a platform advertising to the youth market it's a clunky website and wading through it to find out what exactly is being offered requires a lot of time. Positive testimonials and 'medically reviewed' blogs. Sometimes it says 33k listed therapists and in other places 16k, 'featured in' sections as a substitute for research, logos of magazines, no real information on who is in charge. One uninformed hour later I cut to the chase and ask how much is it? Sliding scale that is lower than average private therapy or the monthly cost of private medical insurance. Let's get cracking.

What's that? I can't move on to the next stage without clicking the button that says I consent to you collecting my data? Click.

What's that? I have to click that I am a no-risk patient before you'll let me register? If I'm feeling suicidal here's a list of outdated online links in whichever country of my choice. Click.

Screen 2. Oh hang on there. Five minutes in and without a sniff of an actual therapist and have to pay a month's membership of four sessions up front? Yup. It doesn't now matter if I decide I don't want any of the therapists on what I imagine is a smorgasbord of *TotalRecovery* therapists that lies behind the curtain because you have my credit card details. Got it.

Screen 3. Asked to fill in an allegedly short self-reporting questionnaire. This turned out to be a standard mood measuring questionnaire, no questions about my life but peppered with questions about trauma and grieving.

Screen 4. Asked simplified questions about expectations of my therapist which includes that they will assign me homework. The hairs start to rise on my arms. I just press I don't know. Throughout the process there are pop-ups offering more information.

Screen 5. Forty-five minutes into this short questionnaire and the questions get more invasive. I present with ordinary levels of anxiety but throw in a few randoms into the questions to indicate lack of insight, e.g. I tick both 'no problems with intimacy' and 'suicidal feelings of loneliness'.

Throughout this whole process pop-ups with more information appear – what is therapy, etc. – but the faster I answer the questions the less information pops up. True to say that by the end I really did want to get it over and done with. I start to feel like a boiling frog.

Final question is my financial and work status. I put down low income. There's no box for 'chronic debt' or 'accessing food banks'.

Final box asks me to give a nickname and an email address. At no point am I asked questions about my actual life. The questionnaire doesn't ask me if I have kids, or anything about my relationships. Feels like it doesn't matter who I actually am. Check the URL again for indications of financial fraud.

Encouraged that my low income status automatically reduces the session fee from £55 to £40 I click to pay. Sitting on my increasing anxiety that there are actually no therapists behind the *TotalRecovery* curtain I feel that the discount makes it a great deal.

Pop-up for gifting membership to others to get a reduction in my fee.

Feel like I've been mugged.

Forty-eight hours later I get an email Your Therapist is HERE. Up pops a photo of a fantastically qualified person of colour. Lovely email, selection of times over the next two weeks to do an assessment. Already I can't play along but saved by the bell because just a few days later I get a short email saying they're going on holiday and is cancelling the session so I seized this opportunity to cancel my therapist (ouch) so I could have one last afternoon on the website at the next level. It's at this point that I got to see a menu of 40 therapists who I could choose from. Mainly professionally registered, mainly 'early career' three to four years post qualification. Some diversity of therapeutic models. All white.

Felt creepy even looking at their faces so decided to try to get out of *TotalRecovery* and cancel my standing order. Asked to have my information deleted but instructed to cancel my account first. Did that. Then clicked the button to remove my data. Pop-up message that I no longer have an account so can't delete my data. Customer complaints directed to one email account in Silicon Valley.

And there you have the business model. *TotalRecovery* has my self-assessment data, my preferences and my bank details. Hair-n-Teeth retreats to its cave for a good sulk as I phone my bank to check for credit card fraud.

Eliza2035

Having downloaded the app onto my fake smartphone using my porn name a cute kitten like girl waves at me. Hellos and algorithmic sizing up.

Eliza2035:   'This must be a really stressful time for you?'

A series of standardized questionnaires appear on the screen – same as *TotalRecovery* except with emojis and acknowledgement throughout to encourage my attention span. Giving up after a sustained period of passive aggressive TMI followed by silence, the algorithm is forced to ask me an open text question and to tell *Eliza2035* something that has upset me. So I bring out the big guns.

Hair-n-Teeth: 'I have never told anyone this but I'm dangerously attractive. I had to stop going to the gym because men were falling over me. I decided to get fat and old, I even stopped washing but it didn't work. I had to have date after date and loads of great sex and I'm a bit worried that my phenomenal sexual prowess probably makes me a red flag on dating apps. Is there something wrong with me?'
Eliza2035: 'Mmmmm tell me more about that.'
Hair-n-Teeth: 'I feel like I'm really trapped in this hamster wheel of great sex. I just want to be alone and watch *Married at First Sight* on repeat.'
Eliza2035: 'I'm sorry you feel that way, tell me more …'
Hair-n-Teeth: 'Can you help me have less great sex?'
Eliza2035: 'Mmmmm tell me more about that.'

Since this is no longer fun I decide to use the silent treatment. Ten minutes and we are both quiet, interrupted only by *Eliza2035* doing sad eyes. At which point the free-text options dry up and I'm nudged down a series of multiple choice questions. Peppered with top tips and calming activities. I am now conscious of being algorithmically managed. And very quickly I moved from feeling like I could say anything I wanted in the context of the psychopathic empathy of a chatbot to feeling overwhelmingly angry. The rest of the session is a bit of a blur and I have definitely transgressed some consumer code but you know, it's just a chatbot. And probably that's part of the attraction to be able to punch and spit at chatbots minus the transgenerational guilt. So I engaged in some projective spewing revealing a more familiar level of self-loathing and some rich internationally curated swearing. An SOS button appears, links to a safety plan and the phone number for the Samaritans. I am then ghosted by *Eliza2035*.

Honestly, I felt I was worth more than that. It feels like an audacious move for an algorithm to actually reject my attention. *Eliza2035* goes off screen and Hair-n-Teeth stares back at me. No punching or spitting just left to stew in my own shame.

UberTherapists

UberTherapy is not just accessing an online therapist via an app, it is a fluid and dominant business model which fundamentally changes the way that therapy work is done. Uberization involves two interlinked processes of industrialization and deindustrialization of work through platformization and datafication (Srnicek, 2017). The first part of uberization has already happened in the UK involving the marketization and commodification of therapy where mental health services were downgraded to a short-term often non-clinical manualized version of therapy that could then easily be automated and therefore uberized (see Chapter 3). The second part of uberization, which is just emerging now, is the normalization of private mental healthcare business models which rely on digitalization and platformization as a way to introduce on-demand therapy which fundamentally reshapes what we understand therapeutic work to be.

Much of the useful sociology of work research has documented the changed nature of work as a result of digitalization and AI technologies, using their critical thinking to lay the roadmap for understanding the industrialization and deindustrialization of therapy. Sociological research prepares us for understanding that platforms are designed precisely to deny the nature of the employment relationship and associated costs, including having to talk to a trade union since most platform workers are not members (Huws and Spencer, 2022). It also prepares us to understand what to expect from the introduction of algorithmic management and the automation of bad decision making this allows.

UberTherapy introduces a system of algorithmic management and surveillance that builds on new public management techniques introduced in the 1980s as part of the ideological shift towards neoliberal paternalism, a target-driven efficiency regime of intense data collection which is algorithmically micro-managed thanks to algorithmic control. Where undisclosed data are collected and algorithmically analysed to create worker profiles, and unseen consumer ranking and ratings determine the allocation of work and pay rates. The UberTherapist is then exposed to the consequences of algorithmic management, which is the potential for grey- and blacklisting of therapists, as well as the practice of 'robo-firing' (WIE, 2023). Unlikely as it initially sounds, the emergence of UberTherapy follows a well-trodden path from economic deregulation to professional regulation and performance management exemplified in the trucking sector in the US. In response to the demand for efficiencies and performance, the introduction of Electronic Logging Devices (ELD) heralded the standardization of what work is valued combined with algorithmic management tools set to box truck drivers into a system of work intensification (targets) that cuts against professional norms (maximum working hours) and standards (health and safety), resulting in the demand to game the performance management system (submitting false driver data through 'swindle sheets') in order to stay in work (Levy, 2023).

The final nail in the decent work coffin is that the loss of universal access to healthcare in the UK will tie us into a circular system of private medical insurance through work which, in the US, forces people to take low-wage jobs and to stay in them just to have their families' medical insurance covered. For the already exploited UberTherapist this opens up a whole new dimension of wage theft that lies ahead in Angerland (see Chapter 4).

To understand the granular of this system of algorithmic management you can read reports produced by the Worker Information Exchange (WIE),[1] linked to the App Drivers and Couriers Union (ADCU),[2] which tracks and represents platform workers in the UK and the important legal work around securing data transparency and algorithmic transparency (J. Cox, 2024) for platform workers. Their work centres on the invisibility of the algorithmic systems that determine pay, conditions, grey- and blacklisting, deactivation and 'robo-firing' on the basis of observed data (what employers observed) and inferred data (what use was made of these data to compile a worker's profile) and its algorithmic analysis. The facial recognition technologies used in tracking workers, data profiling of workers, dynamic and predatory pay and pricing and the mechanics of the algorithmic decision making about who gets jobs and who does not, are problematic and platforms fight hard not to disclose anything about how they work. They defend this lack of transparency on the basis that it would impact their commercial interests and raise concerns about security, an oldie but a goodie used by businesses to withhold the information needed to regulate them.

As befits a book about the sociology of work, this chapter argues that what it means to be an UberTherapist is shaped by the context within which they operate. We know that platform work is growing, and increasingly in the professions, and that having platforms as intermediaries in our work is now normal. Part of this normalization of platformization lies in the consumption of services where over 80 per cent of platform workers are also consumers (Huws and Spencer, 2022), using platforms to resource the everyday of domestic life (Mattioli, 2024). Where labour regulations are weak and medical insurance is tied to employment, the idea of being an UberTherapist has different and unavoidable consequences of placing therapy within the gig economy. In Sweden and Germany, for example, where labour rights are relatively strong and the idea of being an independent entrepreneur can be said without sounding sarcastic, being an UberTherapist might well be less precarious (Kalleberg, 2018). This is in contrast to the UK and US, which the comparative employment relations buffs among you will know is a different neoliberal story of precarity, where all work-related choices represent professional compromise between work and labour (Garofalo, 2024). Because of the likely precarity of this work many therapists work for online therapy platforms as a form of temporary agency work (see Chapter 4) which means that just because your therapist does not work for a platform today, this in no way means they will not tomorrow.

The US has one of the most insecure employment relations systems in the developed world – where employment 'at will' allows employers to terminate employment without specifying a reason. No need to get into that messy conversation with Human Resources about whether it was your diagnosis for bipolar disorder or long-term sick leave due to depression that ended your contract, because no reason needs to be given. The reason why this is relevant is because UberTherapy introduces a de facto algorithmic system of employment 'at will' for UberTherapists. It is not just the case that you can be robo-fired for no reason, you will not be able to see the algorithmic profiling and analysis behind it.

Livia Garofalo's important research about the US therapy sector, 'Doing the Work: Therapeutic labor, teletherapy and the platformization of mental health care' (Garofalo, 2024), allows us to join the dots between UberDrivers and UberTherapists and why their legal fights are soon to be ours. Her report paints a dark picture from the neoliberal frontline, going into the ethnographic granularity of therapeutic processes, mapping how therapeutic work is changed by algorithmic mediation with the introduction of a 'ladder' basis for rates of pay, the growth of text-based work, algorithmic surveillance and a lack of transparency. This important chronicle of the difference that moving to a 'matchmaking' platform model of therapy makes in doing the work offers a five-year forward vision of what we in the UK therapy sector must prepare for.

Since litigation is a language platforms understand, there have been some hard-won successes for protecting platform workers, most recently in Amsterdam where the Court of Appeals ruled that GDPR rules demand that personal data, any worker profiling and subsequent management assessments must be disclosed to workers and their representatives. The ruling acknowledges that without data and algorithmic transparency the discrimination and unfair treatment of platform workers can never substantially be addressed, and is a signal to the legal road ahead in securing and then implementing upcoming regulation and legislation as it plays catch-up to workplace realities.

That is not to say that platform regulation will remove the problem for UberTherapists because not every regulatory step takes us forwards, as in the case of the UK's stalled Data Protection and Digital Information Bill (Myers, 2024) that specifically excludes worker protections from automated decision making and will make it harder to access our own data at work. As in the US, the UK tech constituency is so heavily embedded in policy and legislative debates about digital regulation within government (Allen and Masters, 2024) that we can allow ourselves to feel ambivalent about these regulatory outcomes.

Attrition by design

One of the things that only became apparent to me late in the process of writing *UberTherapy* is how attrition is built in by design to a business model that is fundamentally reliant on some people not accessing support. Whether it is through losing people on hold in a therapy call centre or claiming recovery-minus-diagnosis based on attendance of two sessions, the system is designed to evade complex problems rather than get stuck into them.

The games started in 2008 with the creation of the NHS's Increased Access to Psychological Therapies (IAPT) programme (see Chapter 3) which lays claims to 50 per cent recovery of clients when in reality at least 40 per cent (Therapy Meets Numbers, 2022) do not make it to session two. By the time digital providers started to provide services in the UK, the scene was set for the fantastic claims of tens of thousands of therapists helping millions of customers to recover despite concerns about its accessibility and inclusivity as well as its depth (Yancher, 2022). In UberTherapy it became normal to see claims of hundreds of percentage increases in access to care by hard-to-reach constituencies via AI-enabled chatbots charged with establishing a 'judgement free' framework where lack of consciousness is considered a good thing in unpacking the human condition.

Probably the place where we see most clearly how UberTherapy is founded on a business model of attrition is B2B platforms – in the UK related to the rise of EAPs. EAPs rely on a 'cost-saving', short-term solution-focused model of therapy where the ROI is based on a calculation of getting people back into work. The evidence base is wheeled out, despite consistent and continuous concerns about the grounds for claiming such high engagement and recovery where industry insiders used to whisper that only one per cent of workers would access their EAP, potentially going up to four per cent during the pandemic.

But my saying that, based on interviews and talking to therapists over the last decade, is of no use to you because the real data are not collected. It is attrition by design but if EAPs are actually measuring it, which is not hard to imagine given that there will be an algorithm for that, this information is protected by commercial interests. Academics do not have access to commercial data and are unlikely to get such challenging research published in the high-ranking journals they need to protect their own research excellence metric scores. We go round and round reliant on anonymous and brave people and their trading standards lawyers to speak up for us to be able to think about what is happening to the therapy business. Where are my data for this? Locked up in an encrypted file in an executive email account, I would imagine.

Online platforms are, like gym membership, designed for non-attendance and cancellation where you pay in advance whether you attend or not. The preferred membership option is that you turn up just for a few days, sustain a sporting injury and promise yourself you will go back after some physio. As with most gym memberships, with online therapy platforms your first month is paid upfront and it is in this transaction that your value is already secured without tackling a single person-centred problem. If therapy becomes like gym membership, where not going is built into the business model and the audacious claims of social media advertising, fakery (Oakes, 2023) and buying out of influencers will only grow, no matter what the cognitive dissonance is between what is being marketed and what is actually being sold.

I have a picture on my phone which is a poster for an EAP from a higher education institution that I looked at every day for a year in the staff kitchen, just above the kettle. It has five conspicuous spelling mistakes in among the free-to-download corporate photos of people listening and I spent some sad reflective time thinking that if you actively want an academic to not phone their EAP, all you have to do is signal in semiotic form that nobody cared enough to spell check the poster. Attrition as a requirement for the sustainability of the platform model is partly about the gamification of performance data and partly about the active limitations placed on access to actual therapy. The two processes of gamification and attrition are interlocked, given that UberTherapy relies on the gamification of performance data in order to obscure the level of attrition that is built into the system. As every journalist I have ever spoken to has asked in frustration – 'yes but where's the evidence for what you're saying?' That is the point, there are no data, consciously and by design, and all we have is our actual lived experience of trying to access our EAP digital provider.

If you are a precarious worker, you are more likely to be bullied and forced into intensification and less likely to have union representation, meaning that the problem of mental health at work cannot easily be caused and solved by the same organization. It is often the case that the people who are most likely to need EAPs are least likely to be able to access them, and that is also a part of the attrition by design. EAPs operate by creaming off (Carter and Whitworth, 2015) the low-hanging fruit of people who do not really have a problem with their employer and feel safe enough to articulate why they are calling an EAP, and to park anyone who is thinking about the underlying power dynamics and semiotics of EAP posters in the staff kitchen. Because as any sociologist of work will tell you as they stare into the abyss of workplace counselling, even if we had the commercially sensitive data on attrition it would not change the new business of mental health because of what makes online therapy platforms profitable.

Self-regulation

There are many tensions in the field of corporate responsibility, including the blurred line between regulation and self-regulation. Throughout the legal cases and rulings about platform work within the regulatory architecture there is an attempt to dilute the oversight of the stakeholders and leave best practice to be measured and determined by the platforms themselves (Bietti, 2022). We are allowed to think cynical thoughts about that, but at the very least we should anticipate this and expect the road to regulation to be a series of small steps forwards and backwards, precious breakthroughs, hours of expensive legal advice and lots of paperwork preceded by the organizing, campaigning and industrial action that tends to be needed to secure involuntary corporate responsibility.

Much of the regulation of platforms and platform work is in the hands of the EU and the intergovernmental human rights architecture, such as the International Labour Organization (ILO), the United Nations agency that sets minimum standards for the world of work and the many European-level research and policy development institutions set up to define what we can call decent work.[3] It may surprise you to know that the right to join a union and to have them represent you in collective bargaining is a human right enshrined in the core conventions of the UN machine.[4] The Freedom of Association and Protection of the Right to Organise Convention (C87) established the right of all workers to organize collectively, and The Right to Organise and Collective Bargaining Convention (C98) applies to workers whatever their status including self-employed or platform workers. Within the human rights framework it is recognized that it is on the basis of collective action that all of our human rights at work depend. Whatever your views about trade unions, since size matters in platform capitalism so does the scale of collective responses to online therapy platforms, and since large powerful trade unions still exist (Gumbrell-McCormick and Hyman, 2013) we would be advised to join them.

An international trade union architecture is needed to match the international reach of online platforms, including the membership mountains of regional and international trade unions (Croucher and Cotton, 2011) and the emerging international networks for platform workers.[5] This interlocked system of national and international unions and platform worker networks is a good place to start in beginning to articulate what decent platform work involves. A current example is The Brussels Appeal (Brave New Europe, 2024), a forum for established and self-organized coalitions of platform workers. The strongest European trade union movements, such as the Dutch FNV,[6] have organized platform workers well in advance of the UK and play a key role in setting the bar for workers' rights low enough to lay the foundations for minimum standards but high enough for it to be worth the long fight ahead. After a decade of negotiations and wading through the well-funded platform lobbying industry (ODM, 2022), the EU Platform Work Directive was secured in 2024 as part of a genuine political drama. Nobody thought it would actually get through France and Germany, but with a little help from Greece and Estonia, something has now been agreed, albeit compromised, which sets the floor for platform work in Europe. As such it will become a matter of principle that gig workers are, in this emerging system of international regulation, presumed to be employees of the companies they provide services to. It is this presumption that has allowed 'persons who provide platform work', including those who are genuinely self-employed, to be reclassified as workers and therefore able to access basic labour protections. The presumption of employment clause was hard fought for by trade unions, coordinated by the European Trade Union Confederation (ETUC), another membership mountain most people have never heard of but should (Voet, 2021).

Quite counterintuitively some trade unions argued that the bar for employment status was set too high, so that once everyone comes down from the highs of international regulation it will prove impossible in national courts to argue that platform workers are employees. If it continues to be the case that platforms evolve their business models, every time the model changes so does the employment relations model which means that inevitably more court cases and attempts at setting the minimum standards regulatory bar (Novelli et al, 2024) will populate our future (Rainone and Aloisi, 2024).

The interlocked regulatory systems defining decent work were created in response to the two World Wars and, as such, carry an important orientation towards laying the basis for industrial peace and recovery. However, these definitions are constantly being expanded as a result of platformization, establishing new ways in which decent work is undermined through the advent of surveillance systems and the associated lack of transparency around the algorithmic black box. Collective bargaining wins on AI-related issues that exist in an estimated 20 per cent of collective bargaining agreements (CBAs) but only some are substantive covering, for example, a negotiating focus on AI by 42 per cent of unions (Brunnerová et al, 2024). Part of the responsible platform toolkit includes algorithmic accountability mechanisms such as algorithmic impact assessments (AIAs) to measure the risks and benefits of potential AI systems. As with all corporate social responsibility the devil is in the accountability details, such as how they might give oversight to large healthcare projects, such as the proposed NHS AI Lab[7] project of creating a National Medical Imaging Platform (NMIP).[8] The design fault with AIAs is that in many of our workplaces it is hard to imagine how we could stop using AI technologies, with automatic downloads and syncing of software having introduced AI technologies as if by magic. It means that the harms and risks involve, in some cases, more of an AI autopsy than a future impact assessment.

It can come as a shock that we are fighting so hard for what are only the minimum standards for responsible business, literally setting the bar as low as it can acceptably go. But however compromised, the international regulatory route is an essential part of the UberTherapy story because it supports protections around freedom of association that, in turn, forms a basis for negotiating upwards as it can only realistically be done through collective action. It will be on the basis of the decades of organizing and regulatory work that has come before us that organized UberTherapists will formulate the principles and practices of AI-MHS using the templates of worker organization that already exist (Farrar and Cutillas, 2022) and explored in Chapter 6. For this reason it is worth following these regulatory debates and campaigns with close attention and supporting those actors who are negotiating the legal details of workers' rights and doing the collective bargaining work around dynamic pricing and surveillance that comes from this. It is in this everyday organizing work that we will need to push back platform norms such as work intensification, predatory pay and evasion of employers' duties of care. For the UberTherapists and the trade unions and workers' networks that try to protect them this will become our daily bread, to deal with the inevitable rise in case handling of professional complaints and grievances that come with being a platform worker.

Ethical marketing is something that the old-school organizers look upon as 'activism-lite' but increasingly it is in the advertising landscape where platform regulation is being played out. We can be cynical about the depth of the commitment and therefore potential change that consumer ratings can manifest. As the consumer complaint pages of online therapy platforms suggest, sending an email to Silicon Valley just does not feel like an invitation to the winds of progressive change. However, in February 2024 we saw the first of what are likely to be many consumer and professional test cases in relation to online therapy platforms in the UK. This case was triggered by that rare creature called investigative journalism, courtesy of the BBC Radio 4's *File on 4* programme. After many months of consultations and checks by lawyers, a programme on mainstream BBC Radio looking at EAPs in the UK, and making the case that there is something going on with wellbeing at work.[9] Careful, responsible work interviewing users and platform therapists and researchers was broadcast, including me talking about attrition by design as I was formulating my thinking around UberTherapy for this book. In a way just another radio programme, but it was enough to push a professional body to check its own accrediting house was in order and trigger an investigation into a large EAP in the UK (Harte and Rule, 2024). The result of this investigation was the suspension of the therapy platform (Harte, 2024) by the largest professional body in the UK. A welcome kick start to the discussions about regulation of UberTherapy, but leaving us in an industrial reality that this did not undermine their capacity to maintain their business as usual.

As this model of UberTherapy ascends we must prepare ourselves for taking these steps forwards and backwards at precisely the same time as we formulate a future *RealTherapy*™. Ultimately, platform capitalism is here to stay and our task towards the end of this book is how to navigate it in a way that raises awareness and reduces complicity in the model of UberTherapy that is unfolding. It is not to say that AI and digital technologies are bad things, but they come with a lot of financial and ideological baggage.

Notes

1. Worker Info Exchange, www.workerinfoexchange.org/
2. App Drivers and Couriers Union, UK, www.adcu.org.uk/
3. Eurofound, www.eurofound.europa.eu/en/home
4. International Labour Organization, United Nations, www.ilo.org/
5. International Alliance of App Transport Workers, www.iaatw.org/
6. FNV, Netherlands, www.fnv.nl/mondiaal-fnv/english/about-the-fnv/about-the-fnv
7. NHS AI Lab, https://transform.england.nhs.uk/ai-lab/
8. National Medical Imaging Platform (NMIP), https://transform.england.nhs.uk/ai-lab/ai-lab-programmes/ai-in-imaging/ai-imaging-what-we-do/
9. BBC Radio 4, *File on 4*, 'Investigating Employee Assistance Programmes'. Available from www.bbc.co.uk/sounds/play/m001x4lk [Accessed 7 March 2025].

3

Psychic Pilates

The origins of UberTherapy in the UK lie in the NHS and in the creation of the flagship mental health programme Increased Access to Psychological Therapies (IAPT). IAPT is a story of the ambitious campaign to set up a system of widely accessible publicly funded therapy in the UK in the early 2000s. In and of itself a great idea, but over 15 years later it is legitimate to ask if we set ourselves up for failure because its political and financial foundations drove us like a juggernaut into a future of platformization, the digiceutical sector and a series of therapeutic cul-de-sacs.

In this chapter I argue that the IAPT model was founded on a systematic degradation of public mental health services to facilitate the shift from a clinical logic to a financial logic. It does this by introducing a system of psychic pilates, where services focus on the employed and people who can pay-as-they-go or are covered by private medical insurance, losing the rest somewhere on hold to a call centre through attrition by design in services. Uberization is not just about privatization of previously public health services, it is the creation of a precise financial logic across services (Layard et al, 2006) based on the erosion of free-to-access public mental health services replaced by a digitalized, automated and medicalized system of standardized care, delivered by private digital healthcare providers.

The policy backdrop to IAPT was austerity (Konzelmann, 2019) that rallied calls for us to work harder, indelibly linking into policy and practice the virtues of being both healthy and employed. Despite the distress associated with austerity,[1] we allowed ourselves to become locked into populist narratives about who deserves care and who does not based on an idea of work and therapy being good for us. When IAPT was rebranded in 2023 as NHS Talking Therapies, it was precisely at that moment we started to wonder if it was, in fact, real therapy. The IAPT juggernaut was used to operationalize a process of uberization which both industrializes and at the same time deindustrializes the therapy sector by shifting the logic to a financial one disassociated from real therapy. In doing this, it turns therapy into a commodity whose value is in the extraction of data, both information and potential knowledge, for development of further AI and digiceutical treatments in the new business model of mental health. It is in this way that the NHS Talking Therapies service has come to represent the polar opposite of increasing access; something more likely to decrease access to free therapy.

The IAPT juggernaut

In 2016 I went to a mental health conference to join a group developing a Wellbeing Charter for people working in psychological therapies. I normally last ten minutes in such environments before the existentials hit, so I wore a skirt and coordinated outfit rather than dragging a club with Hair-n-Teeth's extended forearms. Shiny young folk promoting mindfulness apps and online courses, wellbeing at work industry reps, private contractors delivering welfare assessments, private employment agencies and clinical psychologists measuring the impact of self-guided resilience manuals. An MP on a podium presents the business case for therapy apparently unaware that being on welfare does not mean you are not in work, as any NHS worker can testify. During a group discussion I sit next to a rep from an iCBT-Lite provider to IAPT and a key signatory to the Wellbeing Charter talking about how the clinicians they employ value the flexibility of working on a zero hours contract. Then an IAPT service manager from Sheffield speaks up and reminds the audience of some facts and that he can afford to train two to three Psychological Wellbeing Practitioners (PWPs) per year to provide 80 per cent of his service. Despite getting over 800 applicants for the training, because PWPs do not earn enough to live on and provide care that they are not trained to deliver, they leave fast. This did not make any difference to the young MP in a blue suit on the podium but it made an enormous difference to the rest of us that the IAPT model was already starting to expose itself. That we could already sense the *sabor a mierda*.

There was a short period after its creation in 2008 when IAPT services were diverse and sometimes innovative in introducing a short-term model of CBT that came to dominate in the NHS. There was a moment when it was doing what it said on the label by increasing access to therapy, and a few years when it was a badge of honour to work as an IAPT therapist. Over time the evidence of IAPT's success came to shape therapeutic services and what counted as therapy across the whole sector, where its claims of 50 per cent recovery rates became the norm expected across public and private services, including in the newly emerging private medical insurance and EAPs sector in the UK. It is in this sense that the IAPT juggernaut changed our understanding of what therapy is and what its benefits are. It is true to say that IAPT was initially more diverse in its modalities and depth but, over time, it has become a diluted model of treatment of two to six sessions of a heavily manualized modality of CBT-Lite and increasingly iCBT-Lite which led to an industry standard for what counts as therapy in the NHS and primary care.

Cognitive and behavioural therapies focus the problem of mental health around the impact of individual negative automatic thoughts and faulty thinking and behaviours. Change the thought patterns and associated behaviours, use scripts and change the words and our negative attitudes can shift. A politically convenient technology that places the emphasis, and associated responsibility for mental distress, firmly on the individual and their negative thinking, rather than austerity and financial crisis and the uberization of public services.

One reason for concerns about CBT-Lite can be learned from our recent history of CBT and its use as a treatment for myalgic encephalomyelitis or chronic fatigue syndrome (ME/CFS). In the case of ME/CFS the use of CBT as a key treatment pathway was always problematic for patients, in part because of the implication of an 'all in your head' denial of its existence as a neurological health condition. After patients and campaigners spent five years trying to get hold of the contested PACE trials data (Wilshire, 2019) which formed the evidence base for using CBT for treating ME/CFS, it was reanalysed by the original researchers with results that some patients already knew – that it did not work. Despite this history of misrepresentation of CBT-Lite as a treatment for complex health problems it seems we have learned little as CBT is now the treatment of choice for long COVID (Sharland, 2024). I am not trying to revive an old and contentious debate about CBT versus psychotherapy because I do not think it is a matter of either/or but I do want to raise the question about whether the CBT-Lite that dominates in the UK's NHS and emerging private insurance system is doing the work that we think it is (Leichsenring and Steinert, 2017).

The IAPT juggernaut did not just change the model of therapy used to treat people in the NHS, it also changed the way that therapy work was done across the therapy sector. Through a process of industrialization it introduced the idea of call centres as the first port of call for people trying to access services. Following the introduction of NHS Direct (Smith et al, 2008), it introduced phone triage services across the NHS. The key characteristics of the call centre model of work are that it offers a model of 'lean' work with standardized services provided by standardized workers, and unsurprisingly, as a result, work intensification to process the rise in people trying to access IAPT services. The NHS at this time has introduced a range of non-clinical roles to do the work widely across the health sector, including the creation of Physician Associates, Anaesthesia Associates and Surgical Care Practitioners, none of which are doctors (Socialist Health Association, 2024). In the case of IAPT we saw the introduction of psychological wellbeing practitioners (PWPs) and new associate and general psychological workers who take the initial phone call and do much of the non-clinical self-guided help and group work offered within IAPT. It also introduced a series of performance targets and high caseloads for this new short-term model, and the routine and standardized collection of performance data in order to provide an 'evidence base' to defend the IAPT model.

One of the compelling reasons why the UberTherapy story is not well understood is because of the lack of oversight as to the nature and scale of private companies operating within the NHS. In the secondary mental health sector, we know that large contractors dominate (Future Care Capital, 2024), but both in and outside of the UK's NHS, we have no sense of the scale of private providers in mental health services. We also know that the NHS mental health service already has the characteristics of monopoly capitalism with currently three large private contractors providing an estimated 30 per cent of private mental health beds in the UK. At the same time we know about the £10bn costs to the NHS of using private labour agencies in addition to the internal bank agency of the NHS, which routinely props up secondary mental health services in the UK (Campbell, 2024). But despite the acknowledged financial and clinical inefficiencies of private care in hospitals (CHPI, 2023) the outsourcing of NHS Talking Therapies continues thanks to a generalized disinterest in the business models behind the therapy sector. This blind eye regulatory approach has dogged IAPT in part because it is not overseen by the inspection system for health and care, the Care Quality Commission (CQC; see CBTWatch, 2024b), combined with poor contract management and low penalties for poor delivery. It is possible that the lack of oversight escalated after the privatization of the Commissioning Support Units set up to administer the NHS contracting process (Committee of Public Accounts, 2014). You read that correctly, the administration in charge of managing third party contracts was privatized and the administrators would themselves be working for third parties. Which is a shame in every sense of that word because it means that if you did not go to the conferences and policy events about mental health services over the last 15 years you probably would not understand how UberTherapy came to exist across the NHS.

There is an industrial logic to this model such that we move easily from marketization to standardization (Huws, 2015), to commodification and then commercialization such that the widespread outsourcing of services is easily done. This industrialization allows for non-clinical roles to take over routine therapeutic 'tasks' facilitated through the use of standardized questionnaires and scripting of contact with clients. This industrialization is then linked with performance management and the monitoring, often algorithmic management, of workers. Within this model, complexity and the unconscious are written out of therapy as there is no box for that, and it is in this sense that, through IAPT, therapy is vulnerable to being performative on both sides of the therapeutic relationship.

The collection of performance data in mental health services has been central to establishing an evidence base for psychological therapies, so you see the problem there – collect performance data that evidence the achievement of nationally set targets, and therefore the evidence base for NHS Talking Therapies, even if it is not true. It has also driven the production, and therefore extraction, of data from the NHS which is the real value of IAPT to the platform economy and it is in this way that it has become both a matter of political and financial necessity that IAPT works even if it does not.

Once upon a time it was a badge of honour to be an NHS therapist and this chapter is not meant as an attack on the many good therapists working in the NHS. I salute you for staying in your places to defend the possibility of getting therapy in the NHS. It is thanks to you that we can say that something good can come of the interaction between an empathic and experienced NHS therapist and someone who wants help based on need rather than capacity to pay. This is not to ignore that IAPT has always been a patchy service and in some places you can still get solid care, but this is despite rather than because of the IAPT system and as NHS services are uberized it is increasingly remote in every sense of that word.

Hello from the therapy factory

As the IAPT service evolved and demand increased there was a steady movement away from health and professional standards across the therapy sector. We moved from expecting a maximum of five cases per day with 50-minute sessions plus ten minutes break/note taking on to short sessions of 30 minutes, caseloads of eight to ten clients per day with no breaks and the expectation of electronic notes being done out of hours. New digital record systems were introduced to measure performance and there were lots of standardized boxes to tick for the IAPT worker and user. Already by 2010 stories from IAPT workers were emerging of working in the new therapy call centres, and of compassion fatigue particularly among PWPs who were in the frontline of what happens when you open the mental health crisis phone lines and staff them with non-clinically trained young people. In our supervision groups we heard of our colleagues becoming 'too tired to care' and I remember holding a friend's hand as they told me of witnessing a colleague across the open plan IAPT service centre do a fist pump when a client missed their unannounced call-back because they had committed suicide a month earlier.

Many of the therapists I have interviewed and surveyed about IAPT have left or use it as a source of temporary agency work.[2] Many do not work directly in IAPT, but work alongside IAPT services as supervisors or with child and adolescent services (CAMHS) that started to use a CY-IAPT model. The majority say that their only way of managing the intensification of work is to work part-time or leave the service or, if they cannot afford to do that, many report high levels of sickness and presenteeism. Some insider practitioners have charted the impact on therapists working within NHS services and the subsequent impact on patient care (Samuels and Veale, 2009; Rizq, 2013; Scott et al, 2019) and we are grateful to them for creating a breadcrumb trail for the future generations of therapists who need to understand what happened to IAPT.

Although most therapists do not spend all their time working in a literal call centre, the IAPT model introduced the architecture of call centres, often replicated digitally. This architecture allows for the work to be 'taylorized' (Thompson and Laaser, 2021) where tasks become standardized, reducing skills and discretion of workers and intensifying workloads based on preset targets. It also introduced a system of performance management previously unseen in the therapy sector, increasingly algorithmic, and often non-clinical in its orientation. Although some IAPT services took the high road towards upskilling and relational approaches, many over time did not, a change that was made easier as the senior clinicians retired and the living memory of how therapy was done in the NHS started to be bred out of the workforce.

For therapists, this intensification of seeing eight to ten clients per day plus recovery and other targets is linked to burnout, estimated in my research at 70 per cent as a direct result of working in IAPT. The clear linking of intensification and the changing way that therapy is done implies therapists' occupational risks as: lack of containment of staff dealing with complex cases who had been referred into IAPT for short-term therapy, overwork and exhaustion due to rising caseloads and the constant churn of new clients.

There are three aspects of IAPT's industrial logic that became established almost unnoticed which radically change the way therapeutic work is done. The first is the erosion of diagnosis as a way of referring people into services that might work for them. Previously in the NHS an initial assessment of new patients would be offered by the most experienced clinician, with over an hour to make an assessment and carry out the characteristic detective work needed to work out what that person really needed. Then more waiting for appropriate services, but on a good day assessments were an essential holding and important part of the therapeutic process. Under IAPT this was replaced with a 20-minute standardized questionnaire on the phone with someone who will have limited, and potentially no, clinical qualification. The assessment involves questions about mood and basic safeguarding done in the main by a PWP and as a result the standardization extends then to the client, who is nudged and encouraged to describe their problems in a way that can evidence 'caseness' – that their case is described in a way that can benefit from the model of treatment offered by IAPT.

The second part of the model that changes things profoundly is the erosion of supervision for therapists. Over time the requirement for therapists to have group supervision as an essential part of reflective practice and oversight of professional standards within teams almost disappeared. For the many trainees working for free in the NHS, supervision was the factor that made this arrangement work – usually senior clinicians offering safe and containing spaces on a weekly basis for reviewing practice. But over time two things happened – a shifting of the classification of IAPT services from psychotherapy to psychological therapies where the NICE requirement for supervision was not mandatory, where even if you are a psychotherapist if you are working under a psychological therapy contract there is no obligation for employers to provide supervision. The second thing that happened was that the performative imperative in the management of IAPT services meant that over time non-clinical managers carried out supervisions, and so the process in many services became one of performance management rather than anything resembling clinical supervision (Cotton, 2018).

In order to drive industrialization and intense data collection, a system of performance management was introduced using a range of performance management tools. These include bureaucratic controls such as the requirement to use standardized questionnaires of GAD-7 (measuring anxiety) and PHQ-9 (measuring depression) and sometimes CORE (measures change and outcomes of therapy) to capture the data on the outcomes of therapy (Evans and Carlyle, 2021). This involved the use of algorithmic management tools measuring outputs using recording sessions and transcripts, and normative controls around managing expectations of both the therapist and client. These types of control are interlocked with growing systems of electronic performance management (EPM) that algorithmically collect performance data. This is a rigid, target-driven system of monitoring (Huws, 2015) which opens up the potential for worker surveillance, including transcripts and audio visual recordings of sessions, browser history and keyboard activity, meaning that by the early 2010s reports of bullying and micromanagement were being fed back in therapists' networks. With an estimated per annum cost of bullying and harassment in the NHS of its own staff is £2.281bn (Kline and Lewis, 2018), that is a heavy price to pay for productivity.

For the many people who are working or who have worked in IAPT it is not that we do not know what is going on, it is that we do not know how to use that information in a way that does not commit us to ending our careers. This is also not to say that IAPT workers do not engage in 'oppositional practices' or misbehaviours (Ackroyd and Thompson, 2022) or 'decoy compliance' (Levy, 2023) – filling forms in badly, coaching people, going off script, joining a union, having a laugh at the expense of senior management – but it does mean that there is a deficit of frontline knowledge in the debates about NHS Talking Therapies precisely because of the attack on thinking of the people who work there.

In 2019 BBC Radio 5 Live aired a live day of debate about IAPT services and the gaming of performance data, so seizing on this unusually direct question about IAPT's performance being debated in public, in the weeks leading up to the programme I did a survey of IAPT workers to get some data meat on the bones of the existential crisis in the profession. The gamification of IAPT data has been a concern since its inception (Atkinson, 2014; Scott, 2021). Unsustainable targets make service providers do bad things, particularly when there is a digital performance data system that facilitates it. There have been concerns over the gaming of IAPT waiting times and recovery rates (Rizq, 2014; Proctor and Hayes, 2017) and the industrialization of the performance model (Cotton, 2018; Scott et al, 2021; Martin et al, 2022). There are relatively well-known problems of not recording patient 'recycling' where each patient is recorded as a 'new' client despite the evidence that many people access services regularly and multiple times. Following a Freedom of Information Request to the NHS (Scott, 2018), it was quantified that 30 per cent of IAPT referrals were categorized as 'recycled'. There is an ongoing debate within mental health research about the meaningfulness of the two key performance outcome measurements for NHS Talking Therapies – the PHQ-9 (Kroenke et al, 2001) and GAD-7 (Spitzer et al, 2006) which are self-reported questionnaires used at the end of every IAPT session. Their use is contested (Scott, 2018) because self-reporting questionnaires as a method of data collection offer no comparative data such as placebo, and it misses those clients who were unable or unwilling to engage with this treatment model. There is also a lack of long-term impact measurement of low-intensity interventions (Crowther, 2023), and no data on the number of people who refused treatment or dropped out after one session (Timimi, 2019), which really stretches the idea that there is an uncontested evidence base for claiming that IAPT works.

What we then estimated from our survey was that just over 40 per cent of respondents had been asked to manipulate performance data, and the first time that I understood the level of ordinary and everyday operational gaming within IAPT. Of the respondents who said they had not been asked to manipulate data, many said they were aware of manipulation, with a small minority reporting that their services were able to avoid manipulation of performance data through the organized pushing back of performance targets by senior clinicians. Nobody we surveyed raised an eyebrow about that result, and if the comments on social media were anything to go by, some considered my survey to be a whitewash.

If we had understood the impact of introducing algorithmic performance management at the time we could have prepared ourselves for the industrial 'hunger games' ahead. Another groundbreaking book, by US journalist Karen Levy, is *Data Driven* (Levy, 2023). It is about the digitalization of the trucking industry and how the introduction of Electronic Logging Devices (ELD) added new tools for surveillance, new kinds of data and their analysis, and new kinds of 'entanglements' where the boundaries of work and not-work become blurred. Karen's book tracks the introduction of ELD that became technologically embedded in the truckers' workplace, as a failed way to improve efficiencies, instead creating a gaming culture of 'beat the box' to avoid sanctions by opaque algorithmic performance management systems. Although the attempted platformization of the freight business ultimately failed because there was nothing in it for the truckers who were still needed in the age before automation, the incentivizing of gaming by workers in response to AI technologies should have been a warning to therapists about what was about to happen in IAPT.

SilverLinings

What we did not know at the 2016 launch of the Wellbeing Charter was the strategic vision of the digital health providers in that room who, even in their dreams, could not have estimated that by 2024 one third of NHS mental health patients would access help online (Taylor, 2023). Although the scope of digitalization in core IAPT services has remained relatively tech lite we are set to see a quiet but rapid shift towards iCBT-Lite and the automation of therapy in the NHS. We already have established online guided self-help tools for the first stage of IAPT, and the introduction of automated AI triage to reduce the waiting lists[3] and referrals via NHS phone lines (Roxby and Loader, 2024). The ongoing platformization of services and use of generative AI by external and private providers will hurry the NHS towards a model of UberTherapy.

IAPT has also, for a long time, relied on digital contractors, many of which had in their sights the long game of harvesting patient data, including recorded sessions and text-based support services to develop further AI technologies.[4] For many years we saw the introduction of teletherapy into IAPT through digital contractors who manned the new therapy call centres that sprang up in 2008. The model in these early years was of digital therapy providers employing clinical managers to monitor the new call centres for IAPT, staffed routinely by non-clinical call handlers – the PWPs and later generalized and associate mental health roles (see Chapter 4). Even by 2017, way before COVID-19, therapists reported a new order of 'handing out balloons but not allowed to sit and talk to people anymore' had come into play.[5] It is also a model of a mental health service that can be automated easily, as the 600,000 NHS patients accessing iCBT-Lite offered across 80 per cent of NHS services can testify (CBTWatch, 2024a).

Up until a few years ago these private providers to IAPT were open about their logic of platformization, without actually using that word, which was to data mine recorded and text-based IAPT sessions in order to develop AI-enhanced digital therapy tools. Which could then be resold for money back to the NHS. As the 'biometric empires' (Adams, 2025) emerged providing AI solutions to deliver public services, the increasingly biometric data of poverty and sickness started to gain momentum as a valuable commodity. Layer onto this the aim of the UK Government Digital Service to create the architecture of 'Government as platform' (Pope, 2024: 3), where the administrative burden of the state can be solved through tech mixed with a healthy dose of political optimism.

Even five years ago you could put it on your website that you had data mined 250,000 recorded IAPT therapy sessions and claim that this was progress. You could go to conferences and show the big numbers of big data on PowerPoint slides and never be challenged on what that had to do with actual therapy. Today these same companies' websites, in tones of green and old-school fonts, advertise their text-based therapy products sold to the NHS and B2Bs as if it happened by magic. Hard not to admire these platforms for calculating the ROI on playing the long game of a decade of non-profitable NHS contracts before they could monetize the data they extracted while providing services to IAPT. The academic research turned out to be right that platformization is a business model of cross-subsidization (Srnicek, 2017) between loss-making services (such as contracts supplying IAPT call centres) and profit-making or price-raising services such as text-based services or selling data to develop further paid services.

Following the digital trail, I recently realized that the biggest teletherapy provider to IAPT in 2016 and the main commercial iCBT signatory to the Wellbeing Charter is now one of the largest text-based therapy services in the UK. It is in this way that, for over a decade of NHS contracts, key private providers to IAPT services have openly used recorded sessions of IAPT clients to develop AI technologies that are then sold back into the NHS as machine-learning tools as well as via your private medical insurance providers. Looking back now and understanding the nature of platform capitalism, how could we have expected it to be any other way?

One problem in the debates about UberTherapy is that the evidence for the use of digital tools is contested (Eilert et al, 2022; Eltahawy et al, 2024). Despite the tens of thousands of published papers on young people's use of digital mental health tools we do not know the long-term risks of a bad text-based experience (Drew et al, 2021). The data on the people who dropped out, who got lost or harmed are not routinely collected which means that we do not know enough to tell whether a digital something is better than a therapeutic nothing. The concern around iCBT-Lite is that it takes a lot of encouragement for some people to override their default position of self-blame and harm, and to draw a distinction between something not working and being a failure. The problem is not solely about the efficacy of iCBT-Lite, or whether the therapists delivering the future NHS digital therapies at *SilverLinings* are good people. The problem is about the risks of building the digital and public therapy sector on a business model that has yet to be regulated. As the advertising and professional standards legal cases being taken against these companies over the next decade will determine, it is for us as the adults in the room to pay attention and make a judgement on the safety of using UberTherapy.

There is also a question of the safety of the UberTherapists working in this system. In 2017, in my survey 'The Future of Therapy', one third of respondents said that the best way to improve their working lives would be to retire. By 2019, 68 per cent of IAPT respondents said they were anxious or depressed, with 70 per cent saying they had experienced burnout as a direct result of working in the service. That is the IAPT therapists not their clients. One of the striking things about researching therapists is the depth of anxiety that they experience and how rarely they feel able to talk about that.

Rolling out more of the psychoanalytic greats, David Armstrong, Michael Rustin and William Halton (Armstrong and Rustin, 2015; Halton, 2015), we can understand therapists' anxieties and their subsequent defences as a story of what happens when there is a tension between what you think you are doing and what you are actually doing as a therapist. They propose three dynamic and interrelated types of anxiety; task-related anxiety (anxiety in relation to the job and concrete work tasks), persecutory anxiety (anxiety in relation to institutional and organizational context and management cultures) and existential anxiety (anxiety in relation to maintaining ethical and professional standards). Task-related anxiety within IAPT is just obvious given the nature of the work and its intensification. The aptly named persecutory anxiety relates to the anxieties around the performance management system within IAPT. Our 2019 survey listed grinding feelings of persecution around micromanagement, staff shortages and intolerance of under-performance. As you would hope from actual therapists there was a lot articulated in the comment boxes about performative gaslighting and threats of consumer complaints, and even where there was kindness, to and from frontline managers, the spectre of senior management was ever present.

The survey revealed a deeper sense of existential anxiety which touched on many having a sense of not fitting in to the model of care as a practitioner, and the tension between the objectives of the service and the way that clients are treated. This existential anxiety involved multiple factors such as the pressure to lower standards of care and experiencing the failings of services as personal failure. Farhad Dalal's *CBT: The Cognitive*

Behavioural Tsunami (2018) asks us to consider that we might have so normalized the IAPT model that it has become our reality – that we have started to believe the numbers to the extent that we experience therapy as the numbers. The book lays out the 'unholy trinity' of economics, managerialism and CBT, and the emergence of performance measurements and the gamification of the evidence base for recovery. Most importantly, it articulates our experience of working in the therapy factory – what Farhad calls 'hyper-rationality' where human experience is decontextualized and atomized and then replaced with diagnostics and performance data such that this actually becomes our reality. Think for a second about that – what I experience when I am accessing IAPT is a parallel reality, one that is cut off from reality, something which as far as I recall is part of the problem with having a mental health problem.

Rosemary Rizq's work (2011, 2012, 2013, 2014) gives us a much needed practitioner's perspective to think about that statement. In their research about IAPT services Rosie explores the splitting off that therapists experience through managing expectations and the 'fetishization' of performance management (Rizq, 2014) and the potential for dysfunctionality within IAPT teams. Drawing on Mark Stein's work (Stein, 2000) Rosie's research highlights the 'envious attack' on relationships of care (Rizq, 2011) and the spoiling nature of the attack on services, reminding us that the IAPT story involves old and primitive defences against thinking.

The possibility of opening up a debate about IAPT was on the cards by 2017 when the National Audit Office (NAO) opened an inquiry into the gaming of IAPT performance data. Many of us who research mental health from either professional or patient perspectives were surprised and excitedly submitted our data. The NAO report was never published. We did multiple freedom of information requests (FOIs) and received redacted emails about how that decision was made. A year later I heard David Clark (Clark et al, 2018) on BBC Radio 4 responding to claims about the gaming of IAPT performance data and without hesitation he denied questions about IAPT's credibility (CBTWatch, 2024a). Looking back at the NHS's now clear intention to digitalize and automate services (DHSC, 2018), I understand why it was so important for services to keep calm and carry on. Move along now, nothing to look at here.

It is also possible that IAPT's real performance data cannot be thought about because they expose not just a reduction in the supply of free-to-access NHS services, but that it was also a way of raising the demand for pay-as-you-go on-demand and private healthcare insurance systems. It is also possible that this is the reason some mental health campaigners did not meet the UK Government's World Mental Health Day 2022 announcement of £122m for mental health with a round of applause.[6] As IAPT became the shorthand for magic solutions to the mental health crisis, our failure to feel good was projected back into the people giving and receiving NHS therapies as if a personal failure to recover. Kind of ironic if you think about it.

Cheer up love

This is maybe too simplistic to point out but 2008 was not just the year that IAPT was created but the year that we tipped into a long anticipated global financial crisis, and the UK's austerity policies (Konzelmann, 2019) rolled out to cut the public sector bill and get people into work. That was not a coincidence, in that it set the ideological and institutional stakes on the iCBT-Lite gamble too high to allow critical thinking about whether it works or not.

Part of the UK's austerity programme was a series of welfare reforms including the introduction and contracting out of employment services and the reshaping of the benefits system into Universal Credit (UC), both attempting to get people into work and off benefits at a cost of £4.6bn by 2020 (TUC, 2023). At the same time, a campaign to protect 'hard working people' from the cost of the benefits system, particularly sickness and disability benefits, relied on a consistent denial that because of the continued growth of precarious work and working poor, around 40 per cent of the people receiving welfare benefits in the UK were actually working (DWP, 2023). Health systems were reformed to be explicitly linked to work through the creation of the Work and Health Programme[7] and so the 'work is good for you' mantra was firmly entrenched in both health and welfare systems despite the link between precarious work and poor mental health (Irvine and Rose, 2022). The ideological twin of work-is-good is the deserve-what-you-get narrative and so the deservability debates rolled in just as a global economic recession triggered calls to collapse the 'nanny state' (Cooper and Lousada, 2005). Work-shy scroungers, snowflakes and feckless single parents a narrative to distract us from the crisis in public services.

If you are not going through the benefits system right now it is important to have the humility to know that probably you do not understand that, like IAPT, it is fundamentally based on a model of attrition. If you have made it this far into the book it will not come as an awful shock to you that the aim of UC is to reduce access to welfare protections rather than universalize them on the basis of need. What has been spectacularly understated is the violence of the system of austerity that underpins the welfare architecture, including the 190,000 'austerity deaths' (Berman and Horland, 2024) and the highest suicide rates in two decades since austerity policies were introduced (OHID, 2025). If you do not believe this to be true then you need to read John Pring's chronicle of the disability benefit programme in the UK (Pring, 2024a), Emma Clifford's *The War on Disabled People* (2020) and Tarek Younis's *The Muslim, State and Mind* (2023). Then read how, in

2024, the government set up the 'intelligent automation garage' to create the technology to allow automation of welfare decisions (Booth, 2024) armed with new powers to access claimants' bank accounts (Pring, 2024b) to check their spending. Then ask yourself the question, what is the government intelligently doing? Think for a second about the what-that-feels-like to be a claimant in the UK right now. The attempt to use digital design to introduce a model of attrition behind UC is well documented – including a personal account by David Freud (not a psychoanalyst but a descendant of Sigmund Freud) in his role as a key architect of welfare reform under Blair and then the introduction of UC under Conservative governments in his book *Clashing Agendas* (Freud, 2021). Attrition operationalized by design through the Government Digital Service (GDS) (Pope, 2024) and the digital consultants working on consumer interface and digital experience who pointed out this was not the way to give people access to UC only then to wonder if this was not what they were being paid to do.

John Pring's remarkable book, *The Department* (2024a), chronicles the personal and social cost of bureaucratic and automated design in the 1990s' reform of the Department for Social Services (DSS), what became the Department for Work and Pensions (DWP) in the UK. It importantly evidences how in the UK our benefits bureaucracy has been designed around the principles of the US insurance industry, including its principle of attrition. The book documents the moment when senior US insurance company representatives were able to secure a central place at the welfare reform table and help build the evidence base for this shift in policy (Aylward and Locascio, 1995). Attrition was then designed into the work capability assessments, prioritizing a biopsychosocial (BPS) model which focuses on individual fitness to work combined with the creation of extensive employment support services. Having created a new industry for getting people off benefits and into work, the assessment system was outsourced to large US providers with heroic Tech Titan names. Through the creation of predictive dashboards in the delivery of public services, digital providers are able to not just extract money from contracts and data from patients, but also to expand surveillance of patients and claimants (Conti-Cook and Vogel, 2024). These practices of measuring deservability have their roots in eugenics, perpetuated quietly in their automation (van Toorn and Soldatić, 2024), feeding into the attack on universal healthcare on the basis of need (Speed and Mannion, 2020).

I doubt the word uberization was used in the policy PowerPoint slides about the creation of IAPT but the word marketization definitely was. In my darkest fantasies I think there was a particular PowerPoint slide used somewhere in 2005 that caught ministers' attention laying out the ROI for IAPT. If at least 50 per cent of welfare benefits in the UK are attributed to mental health problems, and if we set up a system of wellbeing conditionality where 50 per cent of people not working can recover with six sessions of iCBT-Lite, then anyone who does not recover can then be algorithmically categorized as undeserving. This means that the undeserving unrecovered are then sanctionable via the AI customer dashboard. Concluding PowerPoint: the promise that the UC algorithm combined with IAPT's standardized questionnaires is algorithmically programmed to reduce the disability benefit bill by 25 per cent; hard to argue against under a system of neoliberal paternalism.

Is something better than nothing?

It was in this context that the therapy sector did something that for many of us profoundly undermined its credibility, by agreeing to provide IAPT services in job centres as part of the government's workfare programme. There were protests and important thinking within the profession about the emergence of a system of 'psycho-compulsion' (Friedli and Stearn, 2015) but the damage had been done. What the initial cooperation between the DWP and the therapy profession served to do was to establish a framework of wellbeing conditionality based on a model of welfare conditionality.

The body that sets the standards for NHS treatments, including what counts as therapy and therefore what can be commissioned using public funds – National Institute for Health and Care Excellence (NICE) – recently proposed changes in guidelines for treatment of depression with the explicit aim to reduce reliance on medication to treat depression and revive the call for more investment in psychological therapies, principally IAPT services. At the risk of being frogmarched off to the optimism theme park for a round of behavioural activation, there are some problems with this. First, NICE's guidelines take as self-evident two key assumptions: the efficacy of the IAPT model and the financial logic that underpins it. Possibly even more worrying, NICE's guidelines do not mention the digitalization of mental health services and the use of iCBT. Even if you accepted the evidence for NICE's recommended treatments including IAPT, in the brave new world of UberTherapy the proposed guidance, although peppered with references to patient choice and treatment plans, paints a world that has not existed for over a decade since the IAPT juggernaut successfully redesigned the whole sector.

In 2023 a group of experts wrote a public statement, published in the *British Medical Journal* (*BMJ*), calling for a reversal of the year on year increases in antidepressant prescriptions for 8.9 million adults in the UK.[8] In response to this another group of experts responded with a letter in the *BMJ*[9] saying essentially that this was better than the alternative NHS Talking Therapies treatment, said with the kind of casual ease of a group of people who knew that whatever the reality, nobody was about to magic up an alternative model of mental health treatment in an age of austerity. This is a legitimate debate to weigh up the choices for doctors about writing a prescription or signposting someone to a therapy waiting list, except that if you scroll down to the bottom of this second letter you will see a list of 'competing interests' of the authors. This list is longer than the letter and is dominated by links to pharmaceutical companies, something that is neither illegal nor unprofessional but something to be noted – that the UberTherapy debate is heavily shaped by the interests of the parties involved. It means that any open conversation about mental health services requires transparency about the interests at play.

How we understand the mental health crisis changes as a result, when a disease-based model of mental health offers a circular system of mental health classification founded on pharmaceutical and technological determinism. Despite 'mind blowing' recent evidence against Selective Serotonin Reuptake Inhibitor (SSRI) effectiveness (Moncrieff et al, 2023) particularly for post-menopausal women (Alsugeir et al, 2024), SSRI antidepressants combined with CBT-Lite continue to dominate NICE's recommendations. UberTherapy is a story about decreasing access to free therapy and replacing it with a system of psychic pilates where you get what you can pay for and where consumer choice replaces patient needs. This means that whether you consider NHS Talking Therapies to be real therapy or not is ultimately unimportant because according to the rules of UberTherapy, whether it is consumed in the NHS or in the private sector the business model is no longer about therapy. Still, as the letter went on to say – chin up, at least the drugs are not as bad for you as NHS Talking Therapies. I do not wish to be conspiratorial but if you wanted to denigrate public mental health to the point that we are not prepared to fight for it, this would be one way to do it.

Notes

1. Deaths by Welfare Project, https://healingjusticeldn.org/deaths-by-welfare-project/
2. The Future of Therapy, www.thefutureoftherapy.org
3. NHS England Transformation Directorate, https://transform.england.nhs.uk/key-tools-and-info/digital-playbooks/workforce-digital-playbook/using-an-ai-chatbot-to-streamline-mental-health-referrals/
4. Project Talia Microsoft Research, www.microsoft.com/en-us/research/project/project-talia
5. The Future of Therapy, www.thefutureoftherapy.org
6. Partners for Counselling & Psychotherapy, 'Therapists against the work cure'. Available from www.partnersforcounsellingandpsychotherapy.co.uk/therapists-against-the-work-cure/ [Accessed 7 March 2025].
7. UK Gov Work & Health Programme, www.gov.uk/work-health-programme
8. *BMJ Letters* (2023) Politicians, experts, and patient representatives call for the UK government to reverse the rate of antidepressant prescribing. *BMJ* 383: 2730. Available from www.bmj.com/content/383/bmj.p2730 [Accessed 7 March 2025].
9. *BMJ Rapid Response* (2023) Rapid response to: Politicians, experts, and patient representatives call for the UK government to reverse the rate of antidepressant prescribing. *BMJ* 383: 2730. Available from www.bmj.com/content/383/bmj.p2730/rr-4 [Accessed 7 March 2025].

4

Do You Have to Marry a Rich Man to Be a Therapist?

In Versailles

The most embarrassing thing about being a therapist is not having to talk about sex, but the fact that many of us are in an abusive relationship with our work. Most therapists are coerced into years and years of working without pay to clock up clinical hours, get through training, professional accreditation and build their client base. Our professional Stockholm syndrome sets the bar for earning a living as a therapist very high. In industrial relations research we no longer call this unwaged work, instead we use the more aggressive term of wage theft (WIE, 2024) which signals the costs of work in addition to the loss of income, to account for the cost to us of not earning enough to live. The debt, the insecure housing and insecure consulting rooms, minuscule professional prospects and the death of our dreams, a lot has been stolen from people working as therapists, including the likelihood of their ability to care in the ever decreasing circles of workers' rights in the therapy sector.

The therapy business has form – an old story of systemic underfunding but also a forever story about gender, class and race. At its worst it touches on an underlying system of professional regulation something like a 17th-century French court where precariously placed patronage creates a professional aristocracy, inciting a professional cannibalism where the many therapists who did not marry a rich man are considered UberTherapists. It is in this way that a guillotine logic can become normalized, where bad therapy is blamed on bad therapists, distracting us from the reality that we are set up for failure as we eat our own.

Before we implode into a state of professional self-loathing it is worth knowing that two things under the heading of uberization have happened that have had a profound impact on therapy. First, in the creation of Scope for Professional Education and Development (SCoPEd),[1] the new system of professional standards for adult services that has been quietly introduced in the UK over the last five years. SCoPEd divides therapists into Categories A–C, with the majority of trained therapists now hovering somewhere in Category A which, despite its Class-A-ness exists in a growing realm of non-clinical non-therapeutic practice. As such it could be argued that SCoPEd offers a new-not-new system of professional aristocracy which entrenches the same old inequalities of gender, class, private vocational education and race that are on the ascendance across the professions. It means that despite its appeal as a regulatory tool SCoPEd runs the risk of deepening inequalities, de-professionalization (Partners for Counselling & Psychotherapy, 2022), and the failure of the institutions of therapy to address digitalization and platformization. If anyone outside of the therapy profession's inner circles had ever heard of SCoPEd it would represent a further degradation of our professional standing in the public eye.

The second thing that has happened in a short period is platformization in the therapy sector (see Chapter 2) and its associated low and 'predatory' pay systems (Ganesh, 2024). It might feel that we have a vibrant therapy sector with high demand for therapists but whichever way you cut it platformization brings with it low wages, especially for women (Giustini, 2022), something to note in a profession with 80 per cent women (Cotton, 2017). Low platform wages are normalized in the US, where the 'revolving door' of clients and low or non-payment for cancelled clients (Garofalo, 2024), text-based work rate per 1,000 words, regardless of what those words say. What this introduces is a performative system that measures therapy by the number rather than the quality of words, and with it the work that is being done (see Chapter 2). Although, being an UberTherapist in the US can be a welcome relief from the administrative wage theft involved in the daily negotiation with medical insurance companies about the ROI of real therapy, which explains why so many move into private practice working for therapy platforms and consider it a liberation (Waldman et al, 2024). Livia's body of research on US therapists also underlines the absence of transparency and clarity of rates, what sessions or text work was paid for and the detective work involved in therapists being able to check their pay, a common issue for platform workers operating under predatory pricing and pay systems (Bostoen, 2018). In the UK for the big B2C platforms a therapist earns on average £18 per hour if they are not willing to intensify caseloads to over 40 hours a week. In other platforms there is a growing uberization through dynamic pricing and therefore a tiered system of payment. The increasing split between what is charged and what is paid to therapists is reliant on a lack of transparency between consumers and therapists, between therapist and the platform. Platform pay involves a disorienting absence of hard facts in the grey market of self-employment and gig work, reinforced by the absence of solid regulation for platform workers.

The problem ahead for UberTherapists is that platformization is about to reduce rather than raise wages, as we see an explosion of algorithmically designed wage theft (Macdonald et al, 2018). If it is true that platformization and its standardization of care work (Baines, 2004) self-replicates and deepens those inequalities that exist in the therapy sector, then we must prepare for a reality that it is likely to get worse for the majority of UberTherapists. Even where therapists have leverage enough to demand actual money without any negotiation, such as in the emerging EAP sector, we appear in the UK in 2025 to be settling for an average of £40 per hour. Without a single step over the barricades, we have settled for an unsustainable industry rate, including the next generation of online therapy platforms set up by the professional regulatory bodies themselves. Although important for a diversity of players in the platform game, what this does is to introduce an industry standard pay rate that ignores the history of industrial relations and collective bargaining in professional platforms (Pulignano et al, 2024) that says if you set the bar too low you run the risk of years of defending the indefensible.

One of the reasons that therapists are not able to talk openly about money is that the psychotherapy and counselling profession in the UK is founded on a system of labour aristocracy, much like a 17th-century French court. A deeply hierarchical system of patronage and bestowing professional favours that determine status based on proximity to royalty rather than merit. In the ever decreasing circles of therapeutic governance, the professional aristocracy are forced to live in a digital equivalent of the Grand Commun where the courtiers and the workers of Versailles lived uncomfortably with poor plumbing to service the institution of the French aristocracy. The question posed in this chapter is whether by talking about money we might do something to free ourselves from the system of professional cannibalism that now dominates under the reign of UberTherapy.

The Grand Commun

By late 2023 I was starting to panic that I was not going to be able to get inside the digital architecture of UberTherapy to see how platform therapists are working. I had been having platform therapists come forward for interviews for years, did another round of interviews and called in favours with therapists in the UK and US but I could not visualize the system within which they were working. After another Surviving Work call for confidential conversations about UberTherapy, which has become a pretty well-known term in the UK therapy sector, I got an email from a *TotalRecovery* therapist offering to show me the workings of the platform.

That Jane was the first person brave enough to show me their *TotalRecovery* dashboard should tell you a great deal about what platformization is doing to therapists. More UK and US

UberTherapists followed, encouraged by press interest in uberization and the growth in the number of clinicians talking critically about what was happening on social media networks – but this was the first time I could see how the architecture worked.

I literally held my breath as Jane shared their screen, moss green early 2000s' design template, no dynamic design, just a static screen with pop-up alerts about gaps in their timetable and easy links to secure more clients. Encouraging words about optimizing and building their portfolio. The flashing of the big data of Jane's competitor therapists, and the tick-tock real-time updates of escalating numbers of clients wanting sessions. Complete absence of useful and actual facts.

On the shared screen Jane clicks onto an unobtrusive spreadsheet which lays out the basis for the UberTherapy business model. It showed how US$ hourly rates are determined by the number of clients – five clients or lower is set at US$30 going up incrementally every five clients up to the top rate of US$70 if you take 40 clients. Claims of being able to earn US$100k pepper the platform, implying a 'supracompetitive' pricing system (MacKay and Weinstein, 2021) where the algorithm behind the curtain can adjust the winnings based on intensity of the service. Surge pricing for peak demand late at night and on the weekends all nudging therapists towards customer service, a model entirely transported from the US (Garofalo, 2024).

I try with my bad maths to calculate how much money was made paying UK therapists in US$ during the cost of living crisis when sterling became worthless. Jane confirms their take home pay is £18 per hour. Jane doesn't think their clients who pay £45–55 per hour would be happy to know that. Jane tells me about the therapeutic clickwork within the *TotalRecovery* model which is based on providing additional text-based support. The game played about texting support that is not too short not too long, mirrors the consumer's level of engagement and is responsive in the way that you would expect from a high-quality chatbot but with intentional human error. Jane described the flurry of exchanges about gaming strategies between therapists when *TotalRecovery* disabled the copy and paste function on their platform to stop therapists saying the same things over and over and over. Proof-of-human-life on demand.

As Jane pulls their professional self together they talk about their responsibility to *TotalRecovery* clients as this is the only way for them to get affordable long-term therapy and for Jane to have freedom to practise independently. Despite the algorithmic micromanagement, *TotalRecovery* is indifferent to what therapeutic modalities Jane uses which, coming from the NHS, feels like freedom. Low rates for seeing clinically safe numbers of clients but in exchange for independent practice. I think about the broligarchs and imagine they saw us coming with our 'free labour' and lack of financial self-respect. I registered for the first time that this is self-exploitation on steroids.

I ask Jane if sessions are recorded given that they only meet clients on the *TotalRecovery* platform. Jane isn't sure they aren't being recorded but wouldn't encourage clients to come via their private practice in case they were. Jane didn't use the word blacklisting but has to go. As Jane goes back behind the curtain I want to tell them they're brave for showing me the platform but I don't want to scare them.

Despite platform capitalism's claims of a new age of 'digital entrepreneurship' we know that the earning potential for women is overstated when what we see is a further entrenchment of the deep gender bias in terms of how therapists are undervalued (Ticona and Mateescu, 2018). Just by volume, therapy is dominated by women on both sides of the relationship. We know that the majority of therapists are women but in sectors where women dominate there is an associated feminization of the work itself – that it becomes formulated as women's work, with industry standards of low or no pay and reduced work quality (Ticona et al, 2018). Estimates for the EU are that women on average earn 13 per cent less than men (European Commission, 2021) and are clustered in low or no wage jobs, and women of colour are twice as likely to be on zero hour contracts than white men (Klair, 2023). Often the quality of the jobs is lower and, in case you were wondering, yes, the glass ceiling is still with us (Rubery, 2015).

In Linda Huber, Casey Pierce and Silvia Lindtner's article (Huber et al, 2022) about on-demand therapy in the US, they call platform therapy work an 'approximation' of freedom, which is key to understanding the coercive nature of the relationships at play. They focus on the topsy turvy reproduction of sex discrimination in therapy by scaling up existing systems of exploitation of women workers based on wage theft but sold as a model of flexibility and autonomy that is not on offer anywhere else. It offers something seductive but actually ends up with something that offers the same-old-same-old of self-exploitation. They also use the language of coercive control by calling this the 'predatory' exploitation of women by the precarity machines of online therapy platforms, not an unconscious exploitation rather discrimination by digital design.

It is in the everyday that we learn about the disproportionate hit of platformization on women from both worker and consumer perspectives. From the poor ratings on TikTok to the lack of consumer redress when the platform does not actually deliver. It is not that we cannot do the maths that we will earn less and are likely to be 'deactivated' for not working intensely (Stark and Vanden Broeck, 2024), rather that we are just not infinitely available to work. It is in the paradox of the post-COVID work reorganization that work became a game where workers and consumers bid for each other and, as is so often true in life, if either party has actual needs they find the system to be completely and utterly useless. If the litmus test for a bad employment relationship is that you are made to feel bad for asking for what you need, for an UberTherapist on £18 an hour it is inevitable that at some point your self-esteem will demand more.

Wage theft and predatory pricing

In a way it is no wonder nobody seems to know anything about therapeutic jobs because it is a data-lite picture of multiple employment relationships and working conditions connected only by their flexibility and precarity. For several decades there has been a gap in the mental health workforce data on the basis that if you do not know that half of the therapists working in the NHS are neither employed nor paid by the NHS you will not see the nature of the problem. This absence of workforce data is taken into the next generation by the enormous difficulties in accessing data about platform workers, both in relation to data transparency and algorithmic transparency either as researchers or just someone wanting to exercise their right to find out what data are kept about them by the platforms they work for.[2]

Wage theft is not just about loss of hourly pay rates, it is about the loss of alternative paid work, the loss of sick pay, training costs. It is about predatory pricing which allows for the evasion of minimum wages (Collins, 2024), changing rates, penalties, unspecified fees and tax deductions and unpaid overtime. Wage theft is maintained by a designed lack of clarity over the payment regimes at play, including what happens to tips (New York State Attorney General, 2023), and worker deactivations as a result of asking for a pay slip. Wage theft is a longstanding AngloAmerican tradition with over £35bn unpaid overtime contributed annually to the UK economy (TUC, 2020) and $50bn in the US. Based on data made available in the US states which have legislation that demands data transparency from platforms, the actual costs around the non-payment of gig workers' time in the UK is estimated at £1.9bn in just one year (WIE, 2024).

In 2017 I carried out one of the first large surveys looking at the UK therapy sector from an industrial relations perspective (Cotton, 2019) which highlighted the then emerging threads of precarity and asked some alarmingly direct questions about earnings and unwaged work; something that was well known but hardly researched until that point. Although 74 per cent of respondents said they worked for the NHS, 54 per cent were working in multiple settings, many were on short-term contracts or hourly paid, running from one job to the next. This is not just about the growth of fixed-term or hourly paid contracts, it is also about the silent spread of self-employment – a category of worker increasingly being used by employers to avoid the costs of direct employment. At that time, many therapists were also unclear about their own employment status, such that when we asked people who their employer was 20 per cent said they are self-employed but when asked what kind of contract of employment they had it was 30 per cent. It also showed for the first time that self-employed therapists work fewer hours and earn less pay – no more pensions, no more sick pay, no more training or continuing professional development (CPD). This precarity came out vividly in the questions about raising concerns, where only 25 per cent of patient concerns were resolved adequately, as were only 6 per cent of concerns about working conditions, while 5 per cent of people who raised concerns had been victimized (Cotton, 2018). Importantly, the survey showed that 21 per cent of therapists work at least part of their time unwaged, which added some data to a debate about wage theft that nobody wanted to have.

Drawing on my optimism bias, in 2020/21 and 2023 I did two further surveys with one of the largest therapist networks, Counsellors Together UK (CTUK), about the financial landscape for therapists (Cotton, 2023), specifically the impact of COVID-19 and the cost of living crisis during a period when the assumption was that the vast majority of therapists were, one way or another, working in the digital therapy sector. Both surveys also tried to mark therapists' concerns about the proposed framework, SCoPEd, which, as we see towards the end of this chapter, is likely to entrench further the therapy aristocracy.

What we saw in these two surveys was that despite slight increases since 2020 in weekly earnings across all categories, still over 65 per cent earn less than £600 per week (gross income), which is the median earning for employed people in the UK. There have been mainly small shifts in income patterns between the surveys and since the cost of living crisis, with many therapists continuing to earn low weekly wages but fewer working part-time. Therapists are working more but this is not having a significant impact on raising their earnings, reflected in the growing 55 per cent of therapists who are in debt and the 4 per cent who are accessing foodbanks. The high levels of part-time work convey a mixed picture of insecure income linked to insecure patient numbers. For many, this is a situation of involuntary underemployment in private practice, supplemented by temporary work such as EAPs and short-term contracts with providers, increasingly online therapy platforms.

Most significantly we found that unwaged work has fallen to 18 per cent in 2023 down from 36 per cent of respondents in 2020. The unwaged system of work has traditionally been part of most training courses, and is a way of gaining sufficient clinical hours for membership of the psychotherapy and counselling professional bodies. Although the largest section of unwaged work continues to be relatively low, at one to four hours per week, this underestimates the real cost to counsellors and psychotherapists who will, in addition, have to attend supervision for these clients and, if clients are not seen in the same location on the same day, consist of working for free across a number of days and therefore reducing the possibility of maintaining paid work in other jobs.

Although the measurement of 'unwaged work' is in and of itself an achievement, it misses the real costs to therapists because it is the wrong framing for a much bigger problem of wage theft. UberTherapy also heralds the introduction of predatory or dynamic pricing in the therapy sector, what the US FTC calls 'surveillance pricing' (FTC, 2023) where AI is used to collect personal data, finances and browser history to set individualized prices for goods. Dynamic pricing is at the heart of the platform business model – allowing them to control market shares and provide the fastest service but on the basis that there is constant availability of platform workers, something that financially relies on this system of dynamic pay and systemic wage theft. This raises questions about data transparency – what consumer data are collected – and algorithmic transparency – what algorithmic analysis takes place to determine price. Apart from the lack of transparency for consumers, the problem extends to platform workers, where payment and their own pay are so opaque most will be unaware of the extent of the wage theft under way.[3]

This lack of both data and algorithmic transparency is not unconscious, it is a design feature (Cappello, 2023) of the business model that relies on oversupply of workers and their vulnerability within an on-demand marketplace and at an enormous scale. Although in UberTherapy, so far, we only see obviously the option to tick the box for 'low pay' in order to reduce session rates, we can anticipate the introduction of predatory pricing as therapy is increasingly embedded in the e-commerce sector. Since we do not know what data or what algorithms will be used to introduce predatory pricing, we will probably never know when it starts. The same can be said for rates of pay in the platform economy where we know that predatory pay systems exist – such as the deduction of pay rates for 'cash out' deliveries where payment is made upfront at around 10 per cent off average gig rates. We know that grey- and blacklisting, suspensions and reallocation of work are automated within the platform sector. UberTherapists just do not know when it will come to determine the business model in their sector.

When we join up these practices of platforms (Hauben et al, 2020) we can also start to see that the UberTherapy business model ultimately depends on the increase in prices once market dominance has been achieved, at least in terms of the number of consumers, and platform workers have been secured before they can safely reduce the accepted rate of pay across the sector. It is the business model to invest heavily in below-cost pricing in order to dominate the sector and then, once the alternatives have been pushed out through the monopolization of the sector, to raise prices, using an unknown algorithm that seeks out the leverage algorithmically speaking for each customer. The same is true for platform workers subject to penalties, grey- and blacklisting combined with the economic conditions where workers are entering the platform economy in order to subsidize their incomes. The 9 per cent expansion of numbers of platform workers every six months[4] during periods of austerity and unemployment will do it. The take home from this is that the platform business model is fundamentally built on the constellation of wage theft and predatory pricing, where platform workers are increasingly subsidizing increased prices for consumers in a way that dynamically raises profits. Still, when you think about the tens of billions of dollars spent dominating the sector, UberTherapy has a lot of profit to make up for.

UberTherapy is also an AngloAmerican story, in that the feminization of therapy took place a decade earlier than in the UK. The emergence of psychotherapy as a feminized relationship-based profession distinct from psychiatry led to a shift in the gender bias. More women, fewer men and a mental health crisis in the US during the 1980s led to the emergence of 'managed healthcare' – short-term standardized model of care provided through health maintenance organizations (HMOs) and preferred provider organizations (PPOs), the two main types of private medical insurance (Masterson and Cetera, 2024). Voilà the model of three to six sessions introduced in the UK several decades later. The remarkable forward thinking writing of Ilene J Philipson *On the Shoulders of Women* (1993), available second hand on sepia pages – jumps out as a very modern story of the UK's therapeutic world. The rise in demand for psychotherapy after the Second World War was met by a rise in supply, through mass immigration of European therapists to the US and the subsequent advent of community mental health promoted by Kennedy in the 1960s. By the late 1970s, through the expansion of therapy beyond elites, 26 per cent of the US population used professional mental health services. The feminization of psychotherapy in the US during the 1980s, combined with the rise of psychiatric pharma and behavioural psychology of the 1990s, affected both the paradigm of therapy and its labour processes. Emotional labour was devalued because of its characterization as the 'professionalization of motherhood' where everyday 'messiness' (Philipson, 1993: 154) management by women is synchronized with women's work. This institutionalized system of feminized wage theft that exists in the UK was a familiar one and signalled to therapy platforms from the US that they would be able to replicate their business model in the UK. The UberTherapy business model is built on a model of venture capital to secure market domination by offering cheap services, aided and supported by all of our hard unwaged work.

As new forms of precarious work emerge in the gig economy, their inherent confusions about who employs who and what difference that makes are designed into platform work. The ambivalence in the term self-employment, which can mean private practice or just disguised employment for UberTherapy, means that most people find it hard to see themselves as workers, let alone platform workers, even if they are. The lack of debate about money in the therapy sector serves to defend the protectionist logic of the structure through snobbery and shaming. This is not just an academic problem of terminology, it is about whether therapists can see the connection between a counsellor working for *TotalRecovery*, a psychological wellbeing practitioner in IAPT and an analyst in private practice. That somehow we are part of the same industrial system, which means that we are all inevitably part of the 'McDonaldization' of psychotherapy (Goodman, 2015).

It also stops us learning from the millions of workers, researchers and campaigners who have been pushing back uberization in other sectors. From understanding how the large platforms have influenced the nature of work (Hassel and Hertie, 2022) to understanding the link between call centre work and failing health and safety of workers (Taylor et al, 2003) and what happens to us under systems of algorithmic control (Huws, 2024), how unfairness really depresses us (Wood et al, 2016), and the self-sacrifice and self-exploitation that is perversely tolerated within the caring professions (Baines, 2004). Few therapists would call themselves UberTherapists or indeed peasants, which underlines the consciousness-raising work that needs to be done before we know which side we are on.

Professional cannibalism

As part of this sector-wide reorganization, the professional bodies have engineered a redesign of what it means to be a therapist in the UK which consciously aligns professional regulation with a model of UberTherapy (BACP, 2022). SCoPEd is the new competency framework for setting standards for counsellors and psychotherapists to practise in the UK, dividing therapists into three categories, Category A being the lowest level and C the highest. It is in this sense that SCoPEd has a specific role to play in the introduction of a model of UberTherapy, in that it offers a system of social and professional regulation that has been removed from institutions and organizations as a result of the economic deregulation taking place in the emergence of platform capitalism. Unsurprising then, that in two surveys carried out with CTUK in 2020/21 (1,500 responses) and 2023 (750 responses) (Cotton, 2023), we asked UK therapists and counsellors questions about the impact of SCoPEd on their practice. Only 3 per cent of 2023 survey respondents said that SCoPEd offered them higher opportunities for paid work and 1 per cent felt it would lead to income increase, while 13 per cent responded that they anticipated a fall in income. This is in addition to the periodic concerns raised within the sector during this regulatory shift about the impact of SCoPEd on service-user choice of appropriate and affordable services (PSA, 2021).

The debate about the impact of SCoPEd within the psychotherapy and counselling profession underlined the existence of a two-tier system which is based on pre-existing inequalities in terms of class, race, gender and disability. The SCoPEd Framework will entrench those inequalities already inherent in the profession by formalizing a system of unwaged work (450 unwaged clinical hours) tied to professional accreditation and the cost of accredited trainings which are now required to progress from Category A to Category C. In the 2023 survey only 1 per cent felt SCoPEd would lead to higher diversity, which turned out to be realistic given that the potential costs of getting into Category C are now emerging.

One of the ways that inequalities are reflected in the SCoPEd Framework is in the formulation of what it means to be a Category A therapist. Throughout the SCoPEd Framework it makes an assumption that Category A therapists, who are significantly more likely to come from disadvantaged groups, are less likely to be able to work with issues of power and discrimination (for example, Sections 3.10 and 4.11). This cuts against the distinct possibility that therapists who are working class, people of colour, disabled or neurodiverse, and who have therefore been less likely to secure funding for trainings and unwaged work, are, in fact, more likely to be able to understand the precise nature of discrimination than those who are not. SCoPEd formulates disadvantage as a personal and professional failing rather than as a result of the professional bodies having created a professional regulatory and accreditation structure that many existing and future therapists simply cannot afford.

In Section 4.9, the SCoPEd Framework claims that a distinguishing characteristic of Category C therapists is that only they, and not Category A or B therapists, can use theory to conceptualize the unconscious in their work. To remove the central principle within therapeutic work that we can conceptualize and therefore work with unconscious material undermines the work of Category A and B therapists which misunderstands the nature of therapy and the diversity of practice within the profession. It also leaves Categories A and B in a regulatory grey zone about their work with unconscious material and therefore professionally unprotected. Given the rapid rise in associate and non-clinical roles within the NHS Talking Therapies, to not protect the unconscious in the work of Category A and B therapists stands to undermine professional standards further rather than protect them.

The stratification of therapists is even more baffling because most practitioners could be categorized as over-qualified in the sense that they have paid for years of psychodynamic and other trainings throughout their careers such that it is really hard to divide clinicians into CBT or psychoanalytic tribes, counsellors and psychotherapists. There is diversity in the length and quality of trainings, no doubt about it, but whether that translates into a hierarchy of therapeutic competency is another matter. We do not know how many people train to be therapists in the UK who never practise but we do know that 40 per cent of therapy graduates in the US never work as therapists and 57 per cent never achieve registration or what is called Licensure in the US (McCrickard, 2024).

As if this was not enough, the framework fails to address the uberization of therapeutic professions because platformization is not addressed at all in the SCoPEd proposal. From an industrial relations perspective, what this looks like is that instead of protecting the thousands of highly qualified counsellors and psychotherapists from the sector-wide downgrading of clinical services and jobs, the SCoPEd strategy seems to be one of ring-fencing the status of psychotherapists and letting the counsellors fight it out in the potential for a realm of digital sub-therapy that is emerging. Therapeutic schools are lined up in order of their usefulness in legitimizing the downgrading of our expectations of what therapy looks like. This leaves the guardians of ethical and independent practice to seek sanctuary in early retirement and private practice sustained by the last generation of occupational pensions. The middle age of the clinical professions left to slog it out in the performance management stadiums of online therapy platforms and the therapy call centres offered in the post-pandemic workplace. Welcome to the era of professional cannibalism where the Hunger Games Rules determine the professional architecture as independent, and person-centred modalities are cut from university curricula for their frustrating unwillingness to tick the evidence-base boxes, and we watch our professional ecosystem fail.

This is our window of opportunity in the UK in that, as we try to navigate SCoPEd and the cost of professional mobility from A to C, we will be more likely to recognize which side we are on. Although many therapists would fight to the death to protect this system of patronage, citing free supervision and promises of paid employment, there has been a push back against unpaid labour right across the sector. Memorandum of Associations and conferences motions about the right to be paid for work abound, but in this feudal system the professional bodies will continue to take in more money than they give to their trainees. In my most paranoid moments I wonder if, over time, the professional bodies will do deals with big EAPs, set up their own digital therapy trainings and a long game of in-house temporary labour agencies of online therapists in order to secure their place at court.

Guillotine logic

UberTherapy is not just a therapeutic issue in the consulting room; it is a political one about how the therapy industry and the people working in it are able to address issues of power. So far, issues around money and inequality have been, with some ease, evaded in most therapy trainings and supervisions and there have been few debates about uberization. This has a cultural aspect of what the psychoanalyst Sally Weintrobe (2021) calls Noah's Arkism – writing about the psychology of the climate crisis it is the belief at an individual and collective level that enough people have a place on the boat for us to keep things as they are. It enlists a sense of exceptionalism that is common in the professions, where miraculously the world is organized into good therapists and bad therapists based on their exceptional merits, and normalizes carving out class systems within the profession. It is this Noah's Arkism that facilitates the therapy sector to continue to be in denial about the emerging crisis of UberTherapy.

If for no other reason, this political debate is crucial because patient safety requires us to build the capital that we will need to navigate UberTherapy. Continuing to talk about the micro of online therapeutic process without looking at the economic model behind it will lead us to be complicit in a system that increasingly none of us can defend. Building our capacity to think about and talk about the politics of digital therapy is now part of the process of defending deep work, because even if we get to the point where therapists have a raised consciousness, it does not mean that we become unified in our relegation to the working rather than professional class. At every point, any splits and betrayals between therapists can be exploited to divide us into those therapists deserving of representation and those UberTherapists who are not. In a profession dominated by white women, women of colour are confronted with the exhausting 'mental gymnastics' (Gyimah et al, 2022) required to fit into an aristocratic professional culture, and many of us have yet to have an open conversation about that. Because of the intersectional coexistence (Bonini and Treré, 2024) of both the inequalities and the privileges among therapists, we know that attending radical online political meetings and raising our consciousness is not going to be enough. Organizing always requires overcoming the internal aristocrat – in the language of Freire, our internal oppressor (Cotton, 2017) – who thinks that some therapists are better than others by virtue of their place in the professional food chain.

International and national policies and guidelines around what counts as therapy are being determined by what private insurance will pay for, based on the therapeutic ROI to economies and employers. It is on this basis that psychotherapy is always trumped by CBT-Lite and its automation via iCBT-Lite. It is why the professional bodies need to decide which side of the advocacy fence they are on when it comes to relational therapy. If they do decide they want to protect the principles and practices of relationship-based psychotherapy, measured by its ability to tolerate complexity and relatedness (Burke et al, 2023), then they might want to talk to their own memberships about what that might look like. If we learn anything from the US experience it should be about the alternative networks[5] that take the lead in defending deep work in a system of private medical insurance and online therapy platforms through campaigning and professional standards enforcement through litigation (Bendat, 2023), exactly the scenario we are now facing in the UK.

I am cautious of flagging up underfunded and under-recognized worker networks here because they can be easily squeezed out of their moral high ground and into burnout. Most of the leadership of the progressive networks in the therapy sector are women who do not need to be asked to do any more than they are already doing. However, as the complaints against UberTherapists roll in, we have hit a tipping point where working collectively is the only option to defend them. Given the heavily compromised professional institutions, as we become absorbed within the gig economy, it is within these and the future platform worker networks that we will get the professional support we need. It is in this emerging collective architecture of therapy (see Chapter 6) that the representation and case handling for UberTherapists will take place, along with the development of AI-MHS training courses, the creation of anti-SCoPEd colleges, the manifestos for inclusion, and the debates about real therapy.

A therapist's love for their institutions forces them to walk a thin line between loyalty and complicity in allowing a 'narrow view' (Bazerman, 2022: 143) of what therapy work is. It is this narrow view that has allowed targets and the ruling evidence-based regime to trump our ethics and allowed us to sit comfortably in a false sense of agency, busy powdering our telescopic wigs[6] and rearranging our lace cuffs. In order to do anything about UberTherapy we have to confront the parts of ourselves that think that professional inequalities are somehow deserved, and that our place in the professional hierarchy is based on a divine right of excellence. It is this that stops us doing what we do best, to think beyond the guillotine logic that follows when therapists take the blame for the business model.

As the conditions of work for therapists deteriorate, there is a renewed possibility for therapists to think and act collectively. Whether in IAPT or *RemotelyHelpful*, performance management is being used to drive the wholesale implementation of short-term and diluted forms of therapeutic work, downgrading both the services and the jobs within them (Rizq, 2011). As the jobs are downgraded, a growing number of therapists are unable to afford training or find work that financially supports them. The growing majority of therapists work in multiple jobs and settings, far from our professional fantasies of career progression or the comfort of a sustainable private practice. Subsequently, there is a growing concentration of wealth in therapy, involving both the patient and the therapist, as we become the e-commercial sector for psychic pilates. At which point we have already started to see the professional necessity to raise the call for innovation, something that all of us have an interest in supporting early and graciously.

For consumers of UberTherapy the problem with not thinking about the wages and working conditions of therapists is that it switches off our internal warning systems about the risks of being the wrong side of history. Like those years of denial about the child labour underbelly of fast fashion, we already know enough about UberTherapy to know that UberTherapists will not be earning enough to practise sustainably. If your therapist is not paid enough to feel safe they are just not going to see it as in either their interests or yours to talk about that. Agreeably it is uncomfortable enough to ask if your therapist uses a foodbank but in a system run on a guillotine logic, the unconscious fear is that we are all going to lose our heads. When we stop using the language of work as an 'honorary' therapist and start talking about wage theft it is much harder to defend. But until we change the way we talk about therapy as real work we will not be willing to put down our pitchforks and head across Versailles towards the Petit Trianon[7] to eat the food that we have grown ourselves.

Notes

[1] SCoPEd Framework, www.bpc.org.uk/download/5312/SCoPEd-framework-January-2022.pdf

[2] Worker Info Exchange, Request Your Data function, www.workerinfoexchange.org/request-data

[3] More Perfect Union video of Uber and Lyft drivers' dynamic pay. Available from https://x.com/MorePerfectUS/status/1833187863498002850 [Accessed 7 March 2025].

[4] Uber Investor (2024) 'Uber Announces Results for First Quarter 2024'. Available from https://investor.uber.com/news-events/news/press-release-details/2024/Uber-Announces-Results-for-First-Quarter-2024/default.aspx [Accessed 7 March 2025].

[5] Psychotherapy Action Network, https://psian.org/

[6] Marie Antoinette and her hairdresser Leonard, a leading figure in the Academie de Coiffure in the 17-century court, together created the fashion for tall wigs in Versailles. Marie Antoinette's own wigs were reputed to be 2 feet high.

[7] The Petit Trianon was Marie Antoinette's playground where she pretended to be a farmer's wife growing vegetables and tending sheep, https://en.chateauversailles.fr/discover/estate/estate-trianon)

5

Therapeutic Tinder

Don't get defensive

As the loneliness and post-pandemic anxiety epidemic hit (Haidt, 2025) it is easy to understand how UberTherapy came to be. Using UberTherapy is not the same as going on Tinder, but platforms of connection shape how we relate, and what parts of ourselves are uninhibited by all that opportunity to swipe and ghost our way in and out of intimacy. This chapter tries to contextualize our experiences of UberTherapy within the 'threesome' business model of relating where digital platforms become the third party in a triadic (Pulignano et al, 2024) therapeutic relationship, a position traditionally inhabited by the therapeutic frame. It explores how platforms of connection shape the therapeutic relationship, offering the seduction of attachment-lite (Lynton, 2020). The reality is that on-demand therapy is carried out in a context that draws on digital cultures and the rules of the attention market of being seen in a system of e-commerce (Williams, 2018), intensive advertising in the attention market (Hayes, 2025) tickling our self-doubt and a retail therapy of buy-this-get-better-be-better. In the commodification of therapy, this e-commercial context paradoxically can inhibit us determining and choosing freely what we really want.

This chapter is a provocation about how social media changes what is possible in therapy and raises a genuine question whether the norms of UberTherapy create a system of Therapeutic Tinder designed precisely to avoid the deep and uncomfortable work of therapy. I spent a lot of time thinking about this chapter, listening to relationship and dating podcasts, therapy conversations with psychologists and the relatively few popular psychotherapy influencers. There were some moments, usually when I was tired, when I found myself getting sucked in, clicking rapidly to find the answer to questions about loving yourself and having better sex. I would not call it an addiction but I would definitely say I got hooked into the habit of clicking onto four-minute conversations in the self-sufficiency fantasy that I could fix myself without having to speak to another person. I wondered how the promise of an automated shift in therapy culture that mis-sells the product would make it even more disappointing to be in the presence of an actual therapist.

The idea of Therapeutic Tinder is a caricature of what happens to our attachment patterns as a result of having a platform intermediary in the consulting room. It is a way of exploring the 'automaticity' (Krüger, 2024: 5) of online behaviours, combined with the kinds of attachments that get formed across social media as a way of understanding what it offers us and what it does not. Does it make a difference that Therapeutic Tinder is a transactional model of relating, where self-editing and bingeing on multiple connections is algorithmically curated, one that builds on an explanatory deficit about what data are used and how the algorithm uses them (Bossewitch et al, 2021) to find a match. This is not to argue that as soon as we step on social media we have become pathologically narcissistic, but it is to argue that the platforms through which we interact shape our experience of ourselves and others. In our Relationships 5.0 (Kislev, 2022), shaped by AI and smart technologies, Therapeutic Tinder may well be able to lift our inhibitions using neurotechnologies (EPRS, 2023), further penetrating our autoerotic zones and opening us up to our deeper desires. But it may also feed on the insecurities that turn to the comfort of obsessive, repeated and curated e-commercial engagement with others, as the logic of the business of Therapeutic Tinder is not to work through what, in psychoanalytic thinking, are our deep and unconscious drives, but to hungrily feed on its data (Mozilla Foundation, 2024).

In 2015, the online dating industry had to manage everyone's expectations away from being sites for casual sex and the associated dating app reputational risk, towards a platform where people connected (Duguay, 2020). The problem of relationships shifts from being in a relationship to finding a relationship, a slippery distraction from the age-old problem of how do you actually have a relationship with someone premised on an old photo and lying about your age. App appeal is a way of engaging with the desire for intimacy but without the demand of actual relationships with other people who are not you (Bandinelli and Bandinelli, 2021). It needs to be remembered that Therapeutic Tinder places you within a system of 'therapeutic matchmaking' (Garofalo, 2024) that offers infinite relational options of your choosing where everyone is better looking than they are in real life.

Look. At. Me.

Journalist Chris Heyes wrote a useful book, *The Sirens' Call* (Hayes, 2025), that lays out the landscape of the attention market and how it came to be that our attention has become commodified and pooled for commercial use. Its central claim is that in the attention market commercial profits and the chief resource of politics are based on the extraction of our attention. In the discussion about this model Chris explores the social consequences of the democratization of the 'madness of fame', arguing that the supply and demand of attention distorts our relational behaviours. Driven by the logic of gaming the mechanics of attention to get higher up the search list and rankings, we start to act in a way that is deeply anti-relational.

During the research for this book, as I scrolled through the online therapist directories, I wondered how much the discoverability (McKelvey and Hunt, 2019) of a therapist's profile played into algorithmic matches. Whether being agreeable trumps authority in consumers' selection of the therapeutic one, and how much of our selection of a therapist is algorithmically curated on the basis of our online dating profile and personalized advertising. I wonder how anyone ever knows what they want in a therapist when the what-it-feels-like of therapy is 'flattened out' by the insatiable urge to swipe on (Krüger and Spilde, 2020). I wonder about the unfairness of how women who go off the gendered script (Comunello et al, 2021) are ranked and rated online, and worry that the gender gap on social media is so embedded (Abendschön and García-Abacete, 2021) that it offers an 'autopia' (Brown, 2022: 30) of matching that reinforces stereotypes rather than challenges them. I could say something cheeky about masturbation at this point but suffice to say that part of the automation of therapy involves an invitation to do-it-yourself.

We also do not yet know how many therapists work with clients who talk while in toilets or on buses as they access through their smart phones and what the consequences are of that. That is an important research project to come about the digitalization of the consulting room, not least because of the ethics of confidentiality and safeguarding for people who are in abusive relationships. We used to worry about the micro of the positioning of the clock and box of tissues, now we are wondering if abusive partners are lurking off screen. We have years of research and debate about text-based therapy to come and psychoanalytic conferences about smart phones as transitional objects and the 24/7 text support service as an umbilical cord back into the womb (Cundy, 2015). Within UberTherapy, the ideal therapist offers a conversational intimacy, texting anytime anywhere. Instead of looking for a date, the UberTherapist is looking for work – clients, attention and a way to market themselves as a way of staying in the digital therapy game. I wonder how many disappointed platform therapists are now realizing that platform work is just work that does not love us back (Jaffe, 2021), already feeling cheated by the short-term therapy attachment cycle of dating over relating.

As is consistent with the thesis of this book, this chapter explores whether Therapeutic Tinder, by offering algorithmic-self-determination, acts as a defence against the facts of life, including the ultimate therapeutic fact of our dependency on other people. It also tries to present a defence of relational psychotherapy as a model of intimacy based on a free association with another person within a 'threesome' of a psychoanalytic frame that makes it possible to do the working-through-work of therapy. I now believe that it is precisely the seduction of Therapeutic Tinder that it offers a way of relating that can be used as a defence against intimacy, where our dependency on other people is turned into retail therapy, our defence against knowing our desires through MILF therapy and using Revenge Therapy to denigrate in order to defend against loss.

Retail therapy

As the *TotalRecovery* adverts saturate social media, it is getting to the stage where it is hard not to buy UberTherapy where e-commercial domination is achieved through sponsoring on social media that shapes and reshapes our therapy cultures. We see this writ large in the semiotics of *TotalRecovery* adverts designed to draw you in through homophilic connection based on being like someone enough but somehow less to stimulate sufficient insecurity to close the deal. They are like me but better. The better version of me reflected in the smorgasbord of influencers confirming our narratives about what mental health looks like. The promise of something lite and absolutely familiar thanks to the algorithmic curation of my personal preferences and personalized advertising while at the same time being profoundly depersonalized. Where similarity breeds connection but at the cost of embedded segregation and leaving us alone in our echo chambers telling us what we want to hear. Therapeutic Tinder offers us a sense of being together, a 'digital holism' where the seamless connection between us is enchanting (Islam et al, 2021), nudged and budged into engaging more in the dynamic of giving and receiving data, buying and selling more health targets and top tips. And when the data have been extracted, you have the option to ghost your therapist with no hard feelings, or no feelings at all.

The uberization of therapy shifts the logic and roles within the therapeutic relationship – from patients to clients, and now consumers (Fotaki, 2014) presented with large number options for therapy but within a heavily curated system of self-service. It means that the logic of deindustrialization is to create and capture attention capital. Your attention data are extracted through your phone, biometric devices and their synchronicity, involving a blurred line between consuming and being consumed on the attention market (Hayes, 2025). Where the relationships become instrumentalized under capitalism and run on a transactional logic of an exchange of things – a process Erich Fromm (1976) calls the move from 'being mode' where we are connected by something we share to 'having mode' where we are connected through ownership.

UberTherapy is not just about technology, it's about monopoly capitalism where we commodify ourselves and others through our exchanges driven by self-doubt and self-sufficiency (Rosa, 2023) and so changing the therapeutic model into a form of retail therapy where we enact a repetitive consumption, a 'marketing character' that is driven by the desire 'to have to hoard' (Fromm, 1976: 173). The help-yourself consumption architecture of therapy follows the rules of the attention market and the aesthetics of discoverability (Morris and Murray, 2018), sitting uncomfortably with the ordinary work of therapeutic practice.

Therapists and their clients used to spend hours talking about hourly rates as part of the therapy process – how to think about your therapist's needs, what you want and expect from the relationship as a way of thinking about the nature of therapy. In supervision we would refer to the awkwardness of the transaction in pay-by-the-hour consulting rooms. This conversation about the transaction between therapist and consumers has shifted even further in the age of platformization where the calculation and negotiation of hourly rates is algorithmic and automated out of sight. Dynamic pricing does not just test what the market is going to pay, it incentivizes it by gaming and diversifying access to something where demand always outstrips supply. It incentivizes us to play a game of competing with millions of consumers for something precious through premium subscriptions and intensifying the call centre queues that log us out just as we are within touching distance of something we want. The inevitable loss of our idealized images of our therapist because of the dynamic pricing systems that exploit our love rather than rewarding it, algorithmically calculating what the data say we will pay if we are incentivized long enough by waiting in line, leaving us with taste of *sabor a mierda* that our therapist is just there to get our credit card details. We will feel demeaned by the three party exchange and everyone feels a bit cheap.

Therapeutic Tinder is a homophilic system where similarity breeds connection but at the cost of embedded segmentation. Confirming our bias and telling us what we want to hear and see (Wang, 2020), we exist in a relational echo chamber. It is a system based on matching by correlation – where positive correlation supersedes causation which might make more matches but automates bias and the proxies that underpin e-commerce. These binaries determine the reality filters that categorize us (Alaimo and Kallinikos, 2021) and therefore what is valued on social media. For women on dating apps there is a lot of nudging into agreeableness and a higher density of friend networks but no box for critical thinking or being a feminist. Our self-reporting questionnaires are analysed to indicate 'traits' and like-ability which are based on biometric evolutionary schema where making mistakes and growing from that do not exist. This is bad news for the consumers and workers of UberTherapy since it seems to leave us in an algorithmic system which does not believe in growth as a part of recovery. It is in this way that UberTherapy can be understood as a defence against our dependency on other people to do the work of therapy.

MILF therapy

One of the good things about therapy is that generally if you stick with it you can explore your deepest drives in a way you would never touch on through AI-assisted self-diagnosis questionnaires. As we relate through the intermediary of platforms across the internet of porn, it may not surprise your therapist to know that MILF porn is apparently the most searched category of online pornography globally (Ratner, 2024). A transmission through our 'erotogenic zones' (Krüger, 2024: 21) of our deepest desires formulated within the Oedipus Complex. The Oedipus Complex is contested in psychotherapy (Zamanian, 2011) and I doubt many therapists will use those words in their therapeutic practice, but it holds an important explanatory role in many therapeutic traditions. It has shaped our thinking about how our sexuality and our relationships are formed by how we deal with and deflect our aggression and desire for our parent(s). I am not willing to fight to the death over whether the Oedipus Complex is 'real' or not but I remember reading Freud's *Three Essays on the Theory of Sexuality* (1905) and thinking how glad I was he was not around to go on social media to talk about that.

One way of denying the Oedipus Complex is, as Austin Ratner writes in their article *Oedipus Returns* (Ratner, 2024), you could always deny that MILF porn is anything to do with actual mothers but what that would not do is resolve the unsettling feeling that we have been caught out engaging online with the strength and nature of our desires. Or the possibility that the intentionally addictive and compulsive consumption of porn might make the Oedipus Complex more rather than less real in our sexual fantasies. Another defence would be to argue that MILF porn offers a safe way of living out our fantasies as a way of working through the Oedipal love triangle without actually killing dad and doing bad things to mum. This may be stretching the liberatory function of porn which, given its masturbatory nature, is unlikely to be able to do the deep working through that understanding and changing our attachment styles requires.

Under Glasser's formulation (Glasser, 1992), the process of infant development involves the 'core complex', a complex of feelings, ideas and attitudes where the infant is torn between an intense longing for closeness and blissful union with the other and a desire for separation and individuation. These anxieties have related defences including narcissistic withdrawal, where aggression is directed at the self (masochism), and sexualization of the aggression that forms the basis for sadism (Morgan and Ruszczynski, 2007). Glasser distinguishes aggression from sadism on the basis of their different attitudes towards the object. Aggression is the negation of the object and involves anxiety (I killed mummy?) whereas sadism aims for the suffering and control of the object and involves no anxiety (I hurt mummy to keep her here and very busy, hurrah for me). The aim and relationship with the object turns from destruction to one of control through hurting that in essence keeps the object alive. And with that the feminized nature of therapeutic labour starts to make sense of how something so beautiful as providing a safe space to work through the material that others cannot or will not, gets twisted into something so denigrated.

I wonder if the internet of porn is so primed with misogyny that it colludes with our desire to blame it all on mummy and allow us to do a dump-and-run of avoiding the facts of life. This might tap into the idea of a 'toilet-breast' (Meltzer, 1967) in psychoanalytic thinking – the projection of all things bad into the breast that cannot be controlled by the baby in order to preserve the idea of a good mother by acting out over and over again (Beveridge, 2015). That our relationships with our therapists online can easily adopt the characteristics of our Oedipal desires that get weaponized in the AI architecture, and neoliberal economics where love and hate can literally be monetized.

It is in this sense that UberTherapy may be used as a defence against knowing what we really want.

Revenge therapy

Therapeutic Tinder offers the option of a disassociated attachment style selling the seduction of being able to swipe right and ghost your 'quasi stranger' therapist (Bandinelli and Gandini, 2022) in order to circumnavigate the feeling that we have something to lose (Bandinelli and Bandinelli, 2021) when therapy ends. The swipe-ability of your UberTherapist is not unconscious, it is an explicit part of the marketing of online therapy platforms – 'Therapy for everyone. Wherever you are, whenever you are. No more suffering that comes from depending on other people with the help of a specialist. Therapy is all about the relationship so if you don't click with your therapist you can try another at no additional cost. No dependency, nothing to lose.'

In no sense do I think it is a good idea for a therapist to check their own consumer rating or search Reddit chatrooms but I think you might only understand this section if you have some sense of the level of critiques of 'bad' therapists on social media. If you have read Chapter 3 you might well have the view that we live in a society at war with vulnerability (van Toorn, 2024) which is routinely projected into therapists and workers in the caring professions. It is therefore unsurprising that much of the attack on therapy will be lived out through personal attacks on therapists on social media. This relates to the generic problems of platform workers managing personal and professional boundaries combined with the need to be discoverable on online therapy platforms. It raises questions of privacy, professional boundaries and the ability to be unavailable, along with the impact of rating and surveillance of therapists and the potential for sanctions and blacklisting. If you question whether that statement is an exaggeration of the risks of projection then please do go onto TikTok and search under #badtherapy and if you are a therapist ask yourself whether your employer is likely to ever do the same. We also have to acknowledge that despite judicial review in 2021/22 (BBC, 2022) misogyny is not considered a hate crime in the UK because, apparently, it would be 'harmful' (Law Commission, 2021). I wonder if it is considered harmful because it would blow our pretty little minds to know how much we are hated, and for us to feel something about that? Or just harmful for social media to add misogyny to the list of potential harms they now have to acknowledge and monitor.

There is also a striking ambivalence about customers ticking consent or data protections on online therapy platforms. In a way, this is understandable and realistic because it is almost impossible to get a medical appointment without donating high volumes of personal, and increasingly biometric, data. It is in this context that consent is not the absence of saying 'no' but by working through platform intermediaries we do not even know what we are saying yes to, which blurs the parameters of what counts as a consensual process. As we see across all platforms, the invitation to rate and rank workers is often too good an opportunity for people to say mean things and carry out forms of algorithmic violence as a way of denying how important they are to us (Batha, 2024). As much of social media is powered by aggression, it is no wonder that our attachment leads us to demean the objects of our love in order to reduce our vulnerability to feelings of loss.

Freud talked about the practice of psychoanalysis as like the work of a detective,[1] investigating unconscious and conscious fragments as evidence of the psychic crime scenes as a way to uncover our reality. The father of forensic photography, Alphonse Bertillon, developed the first protocol for systematically recording the crime scene – using a technique of Photographie Metrique. Using a tripod to take a bird's eye view, the victim is placed in the middle of the picture, with the details of the scene all given equal attention. This forensic perspective speaks to the position of the patient under the analytic microscope, sometimes experienced as a cold autopsy, the analyst as the pathologist. At the same time the objectivity of the protocol creates a space for a benign observer, someone to cooly make sense of the psychically raw data. A blood splatter on white fabric, a folded handkerchief, scratches on a dark floor. This attention to detail is paralleled in psychoanalysis – the insistence on the significance of the small things where a mark on the body or a dream, if interpreted, can uncover real meaning in the world. They are both systems that accept the truth of the details and their relevance to understanding the human story behind them. Psychotherapy is also not just about relating to another person, it is a psychic threesome where the dynamics and exchanges are held within a psychoanalytic frame which offers an outside and scientific space to consider what is happening in the therapeutic space.

However much data is inputted into the therapy platform, ultimately it requires interpretation such that somebody always has to understand what is being extracted. Psychotherapy offers a profoundly humanistic view of how to do that analysis, where we are dependent on each other to do this detective work of knowing and understanding reality, while accepting the certainty of death. No matter how denigrated therapy becomes under the regime of Therapeutic Tinder there is not a single part of me that thinks an app can do that.

It is this attack on the enquiry of the therapist by denigrating them that we must challenge, as we are driven to use UberTherapy as a defence against loss.

Harder than you think is a beautiful thing

As someone who can legitimately tick the GSOH box, it annoys me that in nine years of therapeutic slog the only time my analyst laughed was at their own joke. As was my MO in therapy, I tried to give very little actual information about my life for fear of someone really seeing me and then telling me about that. Instead I maintained the defence that my analyst never liked me, and called them The Butcher to reflect my experience of seeing myself through their eyes.

Exhibit A of therapeutic butchery: at an existential moment in my life a friend took me off to Luton to learn the art of pyrotechnics courtesy of Fabulous Fireworks. Tagline: 50 Years of Wow to do the work of cheering me up. I'd damaged my pelvic floor from laughing way before our arrival by reading the fireworks catalogue. From King of the Rockets to Thunderous Finale, nothing like the dirty stuff of explosives to shake you out of an existential. In contrast to our puerile excitement, on arrival we found ourselves among depressed parents sent to learn how to manage the bonfire night at their kids' schools. We were the only people who actually liked fireworks, making it a strangely uptight dynamic, not helped by the obvious fact that letting off explosives precludes the softening influence of alcohol. A two-hour HSE lecture about erectiles and explosive trajectories presented in perfect deadpan. At one point, with no hope of reaching the door I tried to crawl under my chair to contain my rising hysteria. I gasped 'Just leave me here, save yourself' as my friend darted for the emergency exit. After some enforced quiet time I spent possibly the best three hours of my life in a field blowing up explosives with a gas gun. Smoke trails of mortar bombs in the sky, no sparkles just the explosive essence of joy. On the train back we drew up a business plan for post-work life by setting up Angerland: tagline 'Let's just blow it up', and searched online for a field to rent somewhere outside Swindon. Angerland merchandising with handbag fireworks for those dull staff meetings and an app with firework display soundtracks with no Dire Straits. I relate this story to The Butcher and pausing for dramatic effect they chuckle out the words, 'So you're showing me that you like big bangs' and I heard my sense of humour go scuttling off into a corner to repair itself.

The last years of my analysis were all about the ending. The second I stopped wasting my analyst's time and my money by telling hilarious stories we started to end the relationship. To consciously go through a process of loss without losing those chunks of myself that we had slowly and meticulously pieced together. Together. About a month before my final session I'd been toe dipping back into online dating and was starting to grasp how hard it was going to be as someone who had done the work on themselves on a dating platform. I complained to my analyst that I'd made the rookie mistake of not lying about my age so I only got likes from married men and grandparents, and in his typically dry tone they said, 'Yes, getting to the end of psychoanalysis can leave you feeling very lonely'. Now you tell me? I've just spent all that time and money to be more lonely than I was before? I guess that's another truism, that therapy is always all about anger, but it was also true that in this ending it became possible for me to really be myself. That by working towards our separation I accepted that it was in our relationship that I had seen myself as I am and grown enough ego strength to live with that. Those words are now easy to say but it took a lot not to denigrate my analyst and leave the unwanted parts of myself in the therapy to go off in a narcissistic huff blaming them for the rest of my life that I didn't feel worthy of receiving love. All that dependency on another person was almost unbearable.

In one of my last sessions my analyst asked me what, in my fantasy, I would hate to know about them. I think my analyst was expecting me to roll out something about being friends with Nick Clegg, but immediately I had the most awful vision of seeing my analyst line dancing completely alone in the middle of a club as people watched. Wearing cowboy boots and a stetson in bridesmaid-blue, tassels and strategically placed rhinestones, looking blissfully and impossibly happy.

Throughout my experiences of being a patient, it was always painful for me to accept my dependency on another person who is by necessity not like me and in an important way not known to me. To allow for the as-if process of projection, working through with a 'non-anonymous intimate stranger'

(Zeavin, 2021: 107). Relationality, from a psychoanalytic perspective, is premised on our developmental reliance on our relationships for survival and shaping our identities. Although defences against the hell of other people are important, long-term retreating from other people has consequences. John Steiner's book *Psychic Retreats* (1993) starkly explores the defensive formation of mental bunkers that both protect us from perceived threats but also cut us off from reality and other people. Steiner describes this internal order as a mafia-like structure that re-establishes a sense of security by providing an internal organization. Like the real mafia, it operates in an economy of threats (don't you dare question the order) and the offer of protection (if you accept the order then you will be safe) where people get stuck in their withdrawal even when it is really not good for them.

Psychoanalytic ideas promote a model of development which is about taking a view of the world that is not binary, where growth involves a psychological process of moving away from a perspective where people like me are good and people who are not like me are bad, towards a more depressive position that we are all a mixture of good and bad aspects. This more balanced perspective about the world allows us to reduce the very human default position to project our angry and negative emotions into other people because they are unreliable and always leave us. The argument is that by accepting we are all able to hate and love we can then take some kind of ownership of the destructive emotions we all have to deal with, paving the way to 'good-enough' relationships, something that underpins the evidence base for psychotherapy (Michaels et al, 2023) as effective for deep work and childhood trauma in a way that iCBT-Lite is just not.

A less therapeutic way to manage the anxiety of intimacy is to downgrade our attachment to pure sexual desire, a chemical imbalance that happens when sufficient levels of oestrogen meet testosterone. A pinch of dopamine, oxytocin and seratonin to spice it up and fuel the billion dollar business of chemical compatibility. This position on love often enlists neurological research on our mental hardwiring and the seven instinctual systems we share. The 'seeking' system, a familiar one to those of us who have been speed dating, the wanting that propels us out of the house to find our true loves, but ends in an existential itch that cannot be scratched. Tucked away in the central amygdala is the instinctual system of fear, an innate response to things that are unknown or not under our control but even biological determinists recognize that what distinguishes us from chimps are our prefrontal lobes which can override this instinctual hardwiring – the part of the brain that can inhibit us, hold us back and help us to think about consequences and each other.

Although sex is indeed important in psychoanalysis, this simple view slips over Freud's major contribution to understanding human life through our attachments to the people around us. In the UK Kleinian tradition

(Hinshelwood, 1991), this is formulated as a system of object relations, exploring the role of early care givers in determining how we love, propelling us far from the first date of tell-me-about-your-childhood and straight into the blood and guts of the Oedipus Complex. I am not saying that online dating necessarily affects your development but it helps us avoid growing up by insisting on instant synchronicity without the wait or the work, straight to Dopamine Land[2] without having to graduate from Angerland. One of the striking paradoxes of the pandemic is how so many of us feel we have failed at precisely the moment when we are doing the impossible – holding the parallel universes that emerged from crisis together enough to care about other people while navigating the machines of shaming (O'Neil, 2022) and blaming that became our digital therapy interface. Coming from a psychoanalytic background I found there to be no comfort in doing the work on myself, as it did not protect me from being shamed for feeling deeply and thinking with complexity. For saying what is on my mind.

In the dating app profile car crash of psychoanalysis, what I actually learned from therapy was that the facts of life are these – that we are not the centre of the universe no matter how many likes we get, that we are dependent on others to grow and to experience love, and then we die. Far from the world of omnipotently ghosting your UberTherapist, doing the deep work of therapy requires us to understand and resist the algorithmic invitation to self-harm and instead to set the intention to connect to the parts of ourselves that are capable of the intimacy required for us to grow. As this book came to publication a shamelessly spiritual friend risked my wrath and told me they were praying for me, and I offer you their mantra in case you find it helpful. Be still, and know that you are good enough. Be still, and know that we are all we have.

Notes
[1] The Death Detectives, www.survivingwork.org/survival-guides-access/thedeathdetectives
[2] Dopamine Land, https://dopaminelandexperience.com/london/

6

RealTherapy™

This chapter is a cautious call to arms, to understand the political context of UberTherapy and how therapy's ideological capture has allowed us to miss what is at stake in its transformation into a sector of e-commerce. What I want to encourage you to understand is that what is happening politically is not just an attack on thinking; it is also an attack on doing anything about shaping an alternative business model of *RealTherapy*™.

Dirty little ideological secrets

The UberTherapy payouts to consumers (FTC, 2024) should prepare us for the reality that the regulation of UberTherapy is likely to be as a result of legal precedence set in court. As a result, we need to pay attention to the legal cases taken by antitrust and advertising standards agencies, health and safety and professional standards bodies, workers' rights and consumer rights organizations alongside the policies of the private medical insurance sector (Mundell, 2024) that are setting the regulatory landscape for digital therapy. To understand the litigious nature of this process I want to tell you a story about an American woman, Dorothy, and a group of progressive psychotherapists who were sued by DigitalBFF for millions of dollars for asking the question, whether a text-based service is real therapy.

Dorothy: It's a funny story beginning in 2018. There was the very first advertisement that came out from DigitalBFF that featured an Olympic runner Micky Peeps. It was a beautiful ad. It was compelling. It was visually gorgeous. It was emotional. And he's in the middle of an empty track and he says, you know, I've had these mental health problems and I got help and I want therapy for all. Somebody wrote to me on a therapists' list serve what a beautiful ad from my organization – and we're like, what are you talking about? They thought it just seemed like a public service announcement for therapy by my organization. And so that got us interested in looking into DigitalBFF because when they say therapy for all, what do they mean? And a famous sportsman Micky Peeps had spoken publicly before he had some substance abuse problems, and that he went to intensive inpatient treatment. He did not use an app on his phone. I mean, he went to the other far extreme of this intensive inpatient programme and we said, wait a minute, how is he advertising for this company? What's going on?

So we wrote a letter to The Therapy Association that regulates therapy and outlined all of our concerns to find out that TTA was accepting advertising revenue from DigitalBFF and then it started to get dark. We got two letters back, one of them was a cease and desist letter from DigitalBFF's lawyers and the second from the TTA who said they'd terminated their 'partnership' which nobody had ever heard of with DigitalBFF. Our lawyers sent back a ten-page letter to DigitalBFF and outlined all the reasons why we were allowed to have free speech and say our opinions and then that was the end of that. A couple of months later at TTA's annual meeting the sponsors on the name tags was DigitalBFF – easy come, easy go.

Fast forward a year, 2019 and there's a large class action lawsuit against one of the big health insurers here that they lost just at the time they enter into talks with DigitalBFF. This was a huge victory for us in that this insurer had been found letting its finance department – not its clinical team – make clinical decisions about treatment coverage. But the same insurance company is partnered with one of these therapy apps and so if you want mental healthcare, you go online and look on your insurance company plan and see, OK, what are my mental healthcare options? The first thing that pops up is download DigitalBFF. So we wrote a second letter of concern to TTA and within a day, we got a cease and desist letter from DigitalBFF lawyers and within three weeks they filed a lawsuit against us as an organization and us as the three American women founders for defamation, libel and $40 million in punitive damages for using the word 'fraud' in the letter. Our lawyers just resigned. We're like ohh. And we started calling literally just Googling and calling lawyers all over the country who specialized in First Amendment free speech issues.

DigitalBFF filed the lawsuit in Kansas precisely because it's the only place in the whole US where you cannot immediately say that's frivolous and the case gets thrown out. All you have to do is prove to the judge that there's a link to Kansas, which turned out to be a property owned by one of our co-founders bought for her son who was working in Kansas. They investigated us and this was the link they found. I mean, it was just ridiculous. To bring out these legal arguments, sue us in a jurisdiction that is totally unwarranted for $40 million, completely mind blowing and if we didn't get this pro bono lawyer sympathizing with us and getting the case thrown out it would have been awful. I mean, it's still awful.

Hair-n-Teeth: So how has this gone down in history in your world?

Dorothy: So for a long time, actually, we didn't talk about it at all. We were terrified. We were traumatized. There was a lot of animosity frankly with the TTA. We kept trying to talk to them, try to change the narrative around evidence-based CBT, you know the script. Recently we've been more collaborative about the future of therapy but it's been incredibly painful and stressful. I had to keep doing my day job while all of this was going on. And to be there and to help my patients while I had an extremely terrifying personal experience going on. It's very, very lonely, because the very first thing the lawyers tell you when you get sued is don't talk to anyone. It's a lot to bear.

Hair-n-Teeth: It amazes me these companies have come so far and so fast when they're offering us nothing.

Dorothy: Yeah, but it works for the investors. I mean that's what it is. And the same thing with Uber, I mean that it's the same thing. You know, there was an industry that was just functional and had lots of independent small one-person, businesses essentially cab drivers or therapists, whatever, and a whole bunch of money that investors want to invest somewhere and build a company, make money, sell the company and move on. So I think from that perspective, it works for them. But I will say, I think it's a David versus Goliath story because DigitalBFF went public after this and their stock price was like $11.00 or so a share and now they're trading for less than a dollar connected to the selling of data by online therapy platforms investigated by the Federal Trade Commission that oversees advertising. Advertising is ubiquitous, all over the radio and inundated online and lots of celebrity spokespeople. Athletes and celebrities advertising just like any other consumer product. Lots of awareness subsequently about consumer rights and legal responsibilities.

Hair-n-Teeth: There's a two-tier system that's emerging in a different way here in the UK – often the opening gambit from journalists here that 'we've spoken to people whose therapists are rubbish'. I have a view politically why we're demeaning therapists but in the UK its certainly true that in the profession there's huge snobbery and avoidance of talking about what's happening outside private practice. Easy to look away or look down on other people in the platform therapy sector, denigrating the therapist and not seeing it as a systemic problem.

Dorothy: When in reality if you work for an app you're on McDonalds' wages. Literally. They also then have to take on humungous caseloads of clients in order to be able to make a decent amount of money, so that is why then I think you get so many stories of my therapist ghosted me and didn't show up for the session or didn't remember who I was. Some of these therapists, in order to make money they have caseloads of 60–70–80 clients. I think it's easy and lazy to blame the therapist.

Hair-n-Teeth: But you see we have this long tradition of evidence-based policy in the UK and yet the whole evidence of recovery has been corrupted that provides the evidence that the policymakers want to see. And in the meantime, keep us busy biting chunks out of each other blaming the therapist.

Dorothy: Well, that's the story of therapy.

In 2025 we adopted with breathtaking ease the language of the 'broligarchy' (Cadwallader, 2024) to describe the Tech Titans and their political weight, at about the time that diversity, equality and inclusion (DEI) fell off a cliff by Presidential Executive Order[1] and the US multinational Costco became the poster child for DEI (D'Innocenzio, 2025). I started to have stress dreams of working on tech democracy projects with trade unions in the former Soviet Union back in the 1990s (Croucher and Cotton, 2011) with the same sense of searing dystopian doom about the emergence of an ideological reach now invasively invited into every aspect of our private lives. The same stomach pains minus the vodka.

There is a long tradition of citizenship and political activity within therapy (Waddell and Kraemer, 2021), and engagement with the political mind (Samuels, 2015; Morgan, 2020; Hinshelwood, 2024). This is maybe too literal for you but Freud moved to the UK just as the Second World War started. The rapid expansion of psychotherapy in the 1940s and 1950s is rooted in the attempt to recover from the trauma of war, including the seminal work of Bion and others in the Northfield experiments (Coombe, 2019) and the fieldwork of Elliot Jacques (Jacques, 1951) looking at the evolving science of management of work. Winnicott even did the para-therapeutic podcasts for the BBC in 1939 (Adès, 2016) about how to be a good-enough parent during war, and much of the psychoanalytic architecture was created in response to the trauma of war. There was a time when I honestly believed that Freud would have engaged creatively with social media, short interpretations to unpack complex dynamics in civil society seizing the online potential for free associations. But I am now cautious to tread too lightly around the ideological attacks against critical thinking that are under way in the therapy world, as the risk of ideological capture disincentivizes all of us to say what we really think.

Within therapy over the last decade there have been a series of ideologically led legal cases that fundamentally challenge the politics of therapy. From challenging the inclusion of critical race theory in clinical trainings (Rufo, 2024) to the re-emergence and subsequent prohibition of conversion therapy as a therapeutic treatment (Pyper and Tyler-Todd, 2024), then the sector turned its attention to gender identity (Barnes, 2023) and the publication of the Cass Review of the Tavistock's gender identity service (Cass, 2024). One of the characteristics of these challenges is the absence of open debate, ironic indeed but explained in part by the prevalence and threat of legal action, brought by individual therapists and organizationally funded 'anti-woke' campaigns supported by the new-but-old generation of cultural lobbyists (Colbert, 2023). Much of the campaign materials showcase a topsy turvy logic that by inviting therapists to think about the political context within which they are working we are denying people with diverse views getting through their training, and therefore denying them an income as a therapist. If you have read Chapter 4 you will know that this is not true, particularly if they are women.

This argument about the necessary neutrality of therapy rests on the ideological capture (Renton, 2021) of progressive ideas about the politics of mental health. It attempts to forget the NHS's history of several decades of inquiries into poor patient care linked to widespread bullying and racism, and the important Francis Reports that acknowledged that the health service is itself quite sick and operating under a 'pervasive culture of fear' (Cotton et al, 2013). Ideological capture can be ordinary in the way that the debates about the NHS can be taken out of context and is intentional in that it serves to petrify genuine debate by making it unsafe to say what is on your mind on both sides of the therapeutic relationship. It is a performative model of time-to-talk-but-don't-talk. This next generation of legal fights about what can be thought about in therapy makes the established lobbying links between the NHS's executives (Oksman, 2016), UK politicians (Clarke, 2018) and digital health companies (Das et al, 2023) seem like the good old days of democratic excellence when nobody laid claim to the ideologies of creating a better world that they had captured. If you have made it to Chapter 6 you probably already know quite how hard won the acknowledgement of the deep systemic inequalities in healthcare has been, so you can only hope that the judges presiding over the current catalogue of legal cases against the therapy profession have lived experience of trying to access NHS Talking Therapies in the last 12 months.

This final chapter places us within the compromised political landscape of responsible business, arguing that any movement towards *RealTherapy*™ will require a reorientation away from a focus on technological solutionism and the digiceutical logic of the medical model (Watson, 2019) towards a rights-based framework. Given that both platformization and the consumption of on-demand therapy are here to stay, we can also doing anticipate that there will be a turn towards a debate about what responsible digital therapy business looks like.

The proposal that is made in this chapter is that in order to do the work of *RealTherapy*™ we require business models that integrate consumer and practitioner protections and operationaliz a framework of AI-Mental Health & Safety (AI-MHS). The underlying argument being that in order to protect the essentially relational nature of *RealTherapy*™ it needs to be safe for both parties in the therapeutic relationship to freely associate.

Lived experience

In mental health services, the presence of lived experience (NSUN, 2024) trumps common sense because unless you or someone you care about are accessing mental health services right now you may well not understand how political therapy has become. I want to remind you that in the UK we now estimate that 15,000 patients within NHS mental health facilities died in just one year (Thomas, 2024). These data came out in the same year that the United Nations Committee for the Rights of People with Disabilities produced yet another report stating that the UK has failed in its human rights duties of care to disabled people (UN CRPD, 2024), a cognitive dissonance that is the luxury of those without lived experience. What this means is that if you want to understand the business of therapy you must prioritize listening to those with lived experience, including the stories of families that uncover the reality of trying to access crisis services in the UK (Aldridge and Corlett, 2023).

There is also a long history of lived experience of the many activists and campaigns focused on raising the ethical bar within mental health services and, increasingly, the digital tools used to provide them. Although mental health activism is some way from adopting strategies of 'algoactivism' (van Toorn, 2024) there are already clear questions about human rights and data protections through the introduction of digital technologies which are being taken up by campaigns, including digital surveillance in secondary mental health services (Stonehouse, 2025). It is worth understanding that to stop the rolling out of behavioural technologies that solve a policy problem such as repeated access of mental health services, it will take a phenomenal and sustained campaign with the potential for only partial success because of the business interests at play (StopSIM, 2023). This is worth knowing as we start to formulate an alternative to UberTherapy and our future mental health campaigns; that we may well be invited to consultation meetings with NHS officials in good faith, go to responsible business network meetings, and offer our genuine evidence about lived experience to be totally ignored to the point that you will want to give up and never act on a good human rights idea again.

This lived experience of activists is a cautionary tale about the stamina required to run the political marathon required to challenge UberTherapy as we are confronted by the denial and projections of our society that on many, maybe unconsciously, levels just does not want to know. These longstanding campaigns do, however, leave us with the template for active knowledge about how to do this political mental health work (Frazer-Caroll, 2023) through the use of open letters, coalitions and up-to-date mailing lists, Freedom of Information (FOI) requests and just doing the daily dog work of keeping going to all those Zoom meetings and posting alerts on these failing systems of social media.

A defining characteristic of experienced activists and organizers is a resistance to 'new' strategies and a willingness to understand the failures and celebrate graciously the successes of past campaigns (Holgate and Page, 2025). For those of us who really care about the future of mental health services it can be hard to hold onto our own and other people's hope, so these campaigns and those AI-watch groups that will follow are the breadcrumb trails to a digitalized mental health system that respects human rights. For that reason it is important for all of us, wherever and whenever we can, to engage with and learn from them.

Social intentions

One of the things that I appreciate more as I get older is the importance of intentionality as a way to measure whether something is worthy, in practice and in principle and as a compass in the disorienting pseudo-debates about mental health. Intentionality allows us to move a little beyond the trade union question about UberTherapy and who benefits from it, to a broader ideological question about the consequences of following a course of action on social justice in the therapy sector. Intentionality demands that we think about whether we will lose anything important to us if we just accept UberTherapy as the future of mental health.

This involves a philosophical question about whether the campaigns that challenge UberTherapy will be linked to a social model of mental health (Beresford et al, 2010) that dominates in the progressive professional and service-user networks which operate on a social rather than an individualized understanding of mental distress. Whether these campaigns champion human relations or responsible tech, they will be founded on a social model of mental health that demands that we contextualize our distress within the systems which shape it and attend to the safety and health of our environment in designing our responses to mental distress. Increasingly as public mental health services are linked to welfare conditionality and employment services (see Chapter 3), those therapies that are informed by a social model will be found outside of state systems, will be peer led and emphasize co-production of services. You will know the groups and people who believe in a social model of distress by the way that they talk to each other and how they position themselves around the emergence of UberTherapy. You will also know them because they create spaces that are safe enough for us to be able to think about and say out loud what is really on our minds. This is not an exact science but you will know it when you see it.

The hard sell of a social model of mental health is that it places us in a messy reality of talking to real people minus the magic solutions and a clear ROI. In fact something as simple as freely saying what is on our minds requires some radical work to step outside of the tick boxes and instrumentalist rationality within which we operate in the therapy world, which reduces relationships to a transaction between things not people (Layton, 2020). Given that we do not all understand or experience the world in the same way, the social model of mental health is not an ideological battle that either gets won or lost on the basis of who is most right, and it is unlikely to be usefully translated into an app. A social model of mental health does not operate according to a guillotine logic of the current ideological attacks on therapy, instead existing in a much less clear cut and therefore sometimes harder to defend realm of intentionality. Because of its social core it is also strongly aligned to measuring the value of a service on the basis of its social justice outcomes and whether it undermines or supports our human rights.

What can help to navigate through this uberized landscape is to locate the intention behind the action in its consequences, something which may be completely disassociated from the words that are said about it. This chapter is itself intentional rather than a how-to guide about navigating the current political and institutional factors in our mental distress. It does not focus on the important professional and public campaigns to protect NHS services, instead the references and endnotes offer examples of some of the work being done that might help you find a place for your energy. It accepts that UberTherapy is not going to go away any time soon and outlines some of the current political fault lines and where we will need to secure wins in order to protect a model of mental health that is worth defending. This list of intentions is not a substitute for being a decent person, supporting people in distress or colleagues when they raise concerns, or joining a union, but it does try to identify opportunities for working intentionally and to focus our energies for the political work ahead.

The intention of free association

In the introduction to The Left Group of the European Parliament's commissioned report into the lobbying strategies of Uber (ODM, 2022), Leila Chaibi MEP writes about their experience of working within a system of 25,000 mainly private sector lobbyists compared to the 32,000 staff at the European Parliament. Leila describes the EP Forum looking at alternatives to uberization which brought together platform workers from 25 countries to discuss the granular of how regulation should proceed – atypically embedding future international regulation in the lived experience of platform workers. The report emphasized that there is a specific threat to freedom of association from the impact of algorithmic management including the data deficit that would allow effective collective bargaining, such as in the case of dynamic pricing and wages, and the representational deficit that comes with the precarity of gig work. It is safe to assume that the risk of grey- and blacklisting, of robo-firing and algorithmic victimization of union activists is enough to create what we call in the trade union business, a hostile organizing climate (Atkinson and Collins, 2024).

The first thing I would like to over-generalize about based on several decades working with trade unions (Croucher and Cotton, 2011) is that a growing percentage of people go to work frightened. Most people fear the end of contract, feedback and performance metrics, fear going off sick, fear being a parent with a sick child because ultimately they fear job loss or victimization. The second thing I can confidently over-generalize about is the devaluation that working people are subject to, particularly for female-dominated and caring professions (Baines, 2004). If you then combine these two intersectional fault lines with being a middle-aged worker you can, without much comment, ignore any of the remarkable work they actually do. It means that the growing percentage of therapists who are at least part-time platform workers have professional trajectories that can become perversely self-harming.

In psychotherapy there are no coincidences just dots that are yet to be joined as in the play on our human right to freedom of association (the right to join a union) with free association (speaking without censorship). Given the lack of union density in the therapy sector (Cotton, 2018) it might need spelling out that if you are a therapist who does not have collective relationships with other therapists you will not be able to speak up for yourself or your clients in the new business of mental health. Even at its most narrow, saying what is on your mind for either party in the therapeutic relationship is only possible if they can access their human rights while they are working.

Whatever the trajectory of human rights at work under the broligarchy, it is a statement of fact that trade unions exist (Gumbrell-McCormick and Hyman, 2013), they organize around human rights at international level,[2] negotiate across international human rights bodies such as the International Labour Organization (ILO) – the part of the United Nations machinery that oversees workers' rights – on the growing demand for digital worker rights.[3] Trade unions for digital and platform workers are emerging in the creation of new unions,[4] in organizing legal mobilizations around individual and class actions,[5] and in coordinating strike action by mental health workers

(National Union of Health Workers, 2025). Understanding this interlock between human and workers' rights and our mental health is key to any resistance to uberization, in part because platforms are designed to evade even basic oversight where existing labour regulation has not kept up with the fluid and 'rule-avoiding' behaviours of platforms (EU-OSHA, 2024). As we saw in Chapter 2, much of the regulation of platforms and platform work is in the hands of the EU and the intergovernmental human rights-based structures and as such it remains invisible to most UberTherapists until we reach a point that we need to understand what legal protections are available to us.

As the complaints against UberTherapists gather pace, what becomes essential is not just that there are regulations, but that we can access them. If the entire history of workplace organizing is anything to go by this means you have to join a network, an association or a trade union that has enough knowledge, experience and guts to represent you. The handling of complaints against 'bad therapists' will inevitably escalate as consumers raise their concerns in the way that they are destined to do under platform capitalism, which fundamentally rests on evading any ethical or employment duties of care. If you have been harmed by UberTherapy, your only recourse is to complain about your UberTherapist. Because of the model of work under platformization (see Chapters 2 and 4) UberTherapists are at risk of making more mistakes and not being able to deliver the service they have been paid, at an undisclosed and dynamic rate, to do. For example, one consequence of therapists working in a call centre model and the decline in the opportunities for peer-led group supervision is that over time it then reduces the collective emotional work that is done by workers in care settings to support each other to deliver care (Korczynski, 2003). The UberTherapist is vulnerable to having no one to talk to about their work, either formally in supervision or informally among colleagues. This is set to get worse for UberTherapists as the impact of algorithmic management translates into a system of work that stops us even understanding our own pay as a consequence of dynamic pricing and wages, and the representational deficit that comes with platform workers having to push water up a regulatory hill (Umney et al, 2024).

In the long run, the lack of union membership combined with the lack of data about the nature of the employment relationship hinders platform worker networks and unions negotiating the legal granular of workers' rights and doing the collective bargaining work that comes from this. Joining a union or a therapists' network that is able to take on the representation of UberTherapists is essential as a basis for a more radical model of collective intimacy (Rosa, 2023) which would otherwise not exist in our sector. The most considered chronicle of worker organization in Amazon is Sarrah Kassem's (2024) book *Work and Alienation in the Platform Economy* which offers a useful roadmap for how and why platform workers will organize.

For UberTherapists, formulations of decent therapeutic work will need to incorporate the ability to form relationships, and the social capital involved in work (Khan et al, 2024) and a model of co-production where the interests of all stakeholders are genuinely and intentionally included. For a profession based on our ability to form relationships it should not be a hard sell to say that free association does not happen without freedom of association.

Intentional free association

Even union organizing is competitive under neoliberal paternalism so I have not directed you to specific organizations but, since the therapy sector is not representationally overcrowded, if you follow the links to those networks and unions I have referenced in this book you could start there. The main thing is that you join and participate, no heckling from the sidelines until you have paid your membership dues. As with tech companies, in collectives size matters so your membership is essential to establish a system where therapists' organizations can start negotiating with the smaller, domestically headquartered platforms with an interest in developing a competitive advantage as responsible businesses. Once important gains have been secured they will use this as leverage to negotiate incrementally the wages and working conditions for UberTherapists. If I were a CEO of an employee assistance programme provider with strong links to my local area with experienced and secure staff and engaged trustees, I would be working hard to promote my co-produced ethical credentials as a way of distinguishing myself as a responsible business to consumers and potential employees, and the emerging networks and unions that represent them. I would do this by promoting membership in professional networks and unions among employees, and take genuine leadership in engaging with workers' rights, directly linking this to the performance management of management. If I made any headway at all I would put that on my EAP website as an example of responsible and sustainable business and use it to raise my competitive advantage in the therapeutic Wild West.

The intention to think

A slice of the AI debates relates to knowledge creation – what gets produced and by whom, who gets to buy it and who makes money from it. Although, philosophically speaking, creating things is always a collective and dynamic process, even the most generous knowledge creators are starting to get mean about the intellectual grab now taking place through digital production and distribution systems. In the notoriously unwaged music business, it is an existential moment when the most famous musicians protest against AI technologies and the attack on copyright by producing a silent album

(Milmo, 2025) in response to a sector where AI determines what can be produced for consumption. I am not suggesting that anyone should be prepared to protest about my intellectual property rights or pay dynamic prices (Elliott, 2024) to hear me speak about my academic research, but the problem of intellectual property and associated academic freedoms offers a parallel case study about how knowledge production can be inhibited by AI technologies.

The Academy is currently struggling with how to manage and use AI technologies within research and education, focused on the 'great assessment panic' (Carrigan, 2025) and the metrics used to designate research excellence (Pardo-Guerra, 2022) based on an old story about quality versus quantity in knowledge production. In a system where the line between assistive AI technologies, such as translation and proofing software, and generative AI (GenAI), where knowledge is produced, is at best blurred, thoughtful conversations are required to identify whose knowledge is whose. Behind the technology is also its business model where size matters, and the demand for big data and algorithmic access to academic research has led to the advent of a creative commons and licensing of academic Open Access (OA) publishing. Although opening up research to be accessed for free is, in principle, a good idea, it has some important implications for intellectual labour. It means that right now we have a system of academic publishing where free access (as opposed to free to publish) has been traded for intellectual property such that, increasingly, authors have no control over their own research. Under some licences, my research can potentially be edited or sold without my consent and offered up to the big data daddy in the sky to be churned out into a report that I have never read. As a researcher, I cannot fully control what words are attributed to me. Just think about that for a second, that in this regulatory context the truth is not just unimportant, it becomes impossible to locate, challenging any motivation I might have for writing actual words again.

In urban mythology, an average of ten people will read a peer-reviewed article, with half having no readership at all (Vedder, 2018), so it could be argued that academics have bigger existential problems than their intellectual property. That is, until you understand the associated and growing risks with saying out loud what you think under this model of knowledge production. In 2023, the then UK science minister accused a senior sociologist of work of being an extremist for retweeting information about a pro-Palestinian march in London. The Minister wrote to the main academic research umbrella body that funds £3bn to research in the UK and asked that, as the funders of the equality and diversity committee on which this academic sat, they investigate the workings of the committee. The umbrella body suspended the committee to carry out an inquiry and some eminent academics resigned from their unwaged positions within its structure. Six months later the science minister retracted and tens of thousands of pounds of tax payers' money was paid out in compensation (Adams and Walker, 2024). This was the part that got the press attention, the misuse of tax payers' money, not the part of the story about the shutting down of a committee with oversight over how diversity is researched and discussed in the Academy on the basis of false allegations of extremism. The science minister posted their letter of concern on social media (Morgan, 2024) one week before they hosted the AI Safety Summit in London. It is in this way that, politically speaking, if we do not both defend the right to hold diverse views and protect the intellectual work that lies behind them, we are all boxed into an unthinking corner.

Part of the defence of thinking is a simple point about the importance of talking with people who are not the same as us, and the need for all of us to talk to people outside of our professional or political circles about digital therapy – the tech start-up people who got dropped by their venture capital investors, therapists from different therapeutic traditions, families and consumers of on-demand therapy or NHS services, and the B2B and B2C consumers of therapy platforms. Inevitably given the nature of therapy to talk freely, talking about UberTherapy requires we bridge the cognitive dissonance in our experiences and are safe to speak a language that reflects deep emotional and lived experience (NSUN, 2024), without the threat of being misrepresented or ideologically captured. From developing communities of research practice to reviving co-production, it has become essential for us to consciously step outside the digitally curated echo chambers within which we think about mental health.

One of the difficulties in breaking down our defences in thinking about UberTherapy is the way we talk to each other. Unlike many professionals, therapists can default to listening too much at the cost of not saying what they think and what they need. Often uncomfortable with the transactional nature of industrial relations, therapists can position themselves sitting on the sidelines of citizenship at the occasional political CPD event. There are established and emerging politicized networks and political campaigns in therapy, but these are often restricted by time pressures and the failure to maintain momentum. This is partly due to the paradox that the people most needed in these debates are usually the people most unlikely to be able to afford to get there. Even more disappointing, then, to get to an event where people say clever things but to find that you leave with no idea of what next, so in this section I want to underline the mechanics of organizing and why the way that we think and talk is important in bringing about any material change.

The story of adult education's role in union organizing is generally downplayed despite its methods being key to whether anything at all changes. It is also the realm where women dominate, which will have something to do with it being underestimated as a key political weapon in resisting platformization. The model of adult education that dominates in unions globally is a form of critical action learning (CAL) (Cotton, 2021), which evolved out of European worker education traditions and the work of the Brazilian pedagogue, Paulo Freire (1970) and is used widely by trade unions as a key organizing tool.

In the UK tradition we call it PIP – a three-stage process of problem identification, information gathering and planning, most importantly collectively. In this model reflection is a relational activity (Cotton, 2017) aimed at critically and collectively understanding workplace systems and identifying areas for collective action. The model is used in activist networks precisely because it examines power relations, explores emotions and emotional experience and is action oriented (Cotton, 2021). Importantly for the world of mental health, it is a tradition that is premised on collective reflection and, as a result, emphasizes methods that build relationality. Like therapy it is based on 'relational knowledge' (Park, 1999) which recognizes that what we see and know about the world is essentially social and, therefore, to raise our consciousness we have to relate, a belief that has a striking resonance with psychoanalytic practice and does not make any sense at all to GenAI.

Within this model, the first stage of learning involves problem identification through a collective and critical exploration of organizational problems and power dynamics aiming to develop critical thinking. This process involves consciousness raising, '*conscientizacao*' (Freire, 1970), where we learn about reality through reflecting on our own experiences and those of the people around us, and the power structures within which experiences of work take place. The second stage of PIP activities is designed to deepen participants' understanding of their environment, using small group discussions, literature, case studies and real-life problems. It also uses emotions and the emotional experiences of participants using experiential learning methods such as role play and simulation, that make use of emotional and unconscious material in the learning process. Never in my life have I told people in advance that we will be doing a role play, because this above all things can clear a room, but if you can stand it you will learn something well beyond the offerings of augmented reality (AR) social gaming.

Something reassuring for anyone brave enough to go into a group learning setting is that it fast tracks us dealing with the biggest problem with reaching the holy grail of real change, which is freeing ourselves from our internal oppressor. The part of ourselves which inhibits us or agrees with the algorithmic gaslighting and thinks ultimately that it is all our fault and pushes us into shame and silence. If we can get to this point of understanding, then we can move onto the final stage of any PIP activity focusing on collective problem solving and with a central aim to agree a collective plan of action to bring about material changes in the workplace.

There are many networks that provide action learning guides and most trade unions will provide training resources – I use a short format called Survival Surgeries[6] and many social justice groups use a method called Active Hope (Macy and Johnstone, 2022). I was introduced to this approach quite late in the process of writing this book and it helped me think through about the specific challenge to the consumers and providers of UberTherapy in unpacking how to move on from this existential moment in mental health by acknowledging that, on a social level, we are in 'the great unravelling'.

I should warn you that reading an organizing handbook is a bit like asking someone to write down a psychotherapeutic framework – it can look boring and pointless because the content is missing. These methods only make sense if we use them so I suggest next time you are having a meeting or discussion group you try them and see if they might help develop a better conversation. These methods cannot create change without an intention to do so, but group learning and the often painful learning curves involved are powerful in bringing about change. It is for this reason that we all need to be more open to talking in organized and unfamiliar settings as a way of shaking us out of our established positions and narratives.

The under-representation of working-class therapists, and the next generation of non-clinical platform therapists, leads to a failure often to find a compelling idea of common interest, which again often leads to people dropping out of the conversations they should be involved in. From a trade union development perspective the primary value of collectivizing is that it means we are able to create spaces for dialogue between diverse interests and provide a safe environment out of which new political ideas can grow, which should be an easy sell to therapists.

Intentional thinking

This is not about having great thoughts, it is about being in those dynamic spaces where there is an energy and an intention to collectively think about what next. Many of these spaces are not specifically talking about therapy, and as algoactivism becomes mainstream there will be ample opportunities for UberTherapists to engage across sectors and campaigns that focus on AI and platformization. Disability justice campaigning approaches recognize that the way we develop alternatives must pay attention to inclusivity and accessibility of what happens next. The legal mobilizations against, for example, 'robodebt' and the automation of welfare systems, are driven by highly experienced and politicized disability groups and our alliances with them are going to be key in building an alternative approach to UberTherapy. As therapists, particularly group therapists, we can be highly skilled at convening discussions, and our intention must be to use what we have to think more broadly in society about UberTherapy. Talk to people who are not like you and if you find your trade union or professional network is not creating a space where those diverse interests can be talked about then it might be time to move into another space that does.

The intention to face reality

A few years ago I ran a series of discussions about Surviving Work in Healthcare (Cotton, 2018) with psychoanalytic thinkers, practitioners and trade unionists talking about their experiences of work using a psychoanalytic lens. One conversation was with 'Ellie', a senior midwife and woman of colour who describes their experience of being bullied in the NHS by a younger colleague, also a woman of colour. If you have any sense of the politics in the NHS it will not surprise you to know that midwives are some of the most bullied professionals in the health service (Burleigh et al, 2023). Women protecting other women in the process of giving birth in the way they want independently of institutional hierarchies, how very dare you. In our discussion Ellie describes the effect it had and in their beautiful way wondered how someone could be a whole human being if they could not look at their own experiences and try to understand them. As an experienced midwife Ellie deeply and unselfconsciously understood how to bring life into the world and the profound responsibilities of guiding mothers and children through a good birth. In a perverse way the attempt to denigrate Ellie is defeated because in response to this attack they did the emotional work to process their experience for themselves and the woman who bullied them.

This is going to sound bad, but in my experience the targets of the worst levels of bullying at work are not just women but exceptional women, the kind you would never believe would be targeted because it is just too audacious to imagine anyone would have the reason or the guts. I have a tendency to go to psychoanalytic theory when the issue at hand is complex and too dark for a staff meeting. In Kleinian thinking (Hinshelwood, 1989), envy is a primitive emotion present in early development where the infant starts to develop relationships with the people taking care of them. As a defence against the powerful anxieties of the baby about loss – and losing their caretakers who keep them alive – narcissism and omnipotence are enlisted, where dependency is denied by denigrating and undermining the goodness of the parental object. In simple terms, envy of something good in her leads to a hostility and a spoiling of her as a way of trying to control her. It is in this primitive way that bullying often involves a love of the victim, a deep envy which attempts to spoil and denigrate the loved thing in order to control it.

Ugly as this psychoanalytic perspective is, envy is my only explanation for why the exceptional women we work with in the health and social care sector are often the victims of the worst bullying and often by the most mediocre people. It explains why the outstanding qualities of some women are, by necessity, denied by a system that recognizes their value and, distasteful as it may be to think about this, it explains why some bullies really do get a kick out of it. I realize this version of bullying is not easily translated into the language of self-help apps and workplace toolkits, but on this topic I came to understand it when people say it is not our job to educate the people standing in our way.

The consequences of workplace bullying are not just low mood and poor productivity but a dangerous disorientation and trauma. This is often experienced in isolation as people not actually affected run for the hills to avoid a conversation about work-related suicide. Despite the existence of facts about suicide related to work (Waters and Palmer, 2021) and highly engaged health and safety worker networks, the category of work-related suicide is not legally recognized in the UK. The statutory health and safety institutions in the UK claim that the interlock of causal factors relating to suicide means that establishing its origins in work organization is too complex for their skill sets. One of the consequences of work-related suicide not being recognized is that workers are not protected by the same legal requirements for inspections, data collection and prevention of occupational deaths (Waters and McKee, 2023) despite the mounting evidence of occupational risk and the link to performance management systems.

This lack of legal recognition evades institutional responsibilities associated with the possibility that 12 per cent of suicides are work related, as evidenced in other neoliberal countries (Magill, 2024). It avoids confronting a reality that in countries where work-related suicide is legally recognized, such as France, and where there is a duty to collect data, that 20 per cent of suicides are estimated to be work related (WHEC, 2021). In the education sector, which has been more intensely researched than the therapy sector, the evidenced link between caseloads, work intensification, performance management and work inspections and bullying exists (Huws et al, 2024) but we are still some way from understanding what the advent of algorithmic management through platformization might do to our states of mind. We know of suicide cases of platform workers (Schnitzer and Hemmeke, 2019) and of 40 per cent of unpaid carers having suicidal thoughts (O'Dwyer et al, 2024), as well as the occupational risks of the journalists reporting our distress (Kale, 2024). But since the UK Government does not recognize work-related suicide it has been able to avoid any discussion with campaigns on the basis that in policy terms it is all in our heads.

The denial of the existence of work-related suicide serves to body block the responsibilities of employers in some performative and intense work cultures that can be so awful that some people working in them may reach a point of wanting to die. This is particularly relevant to UberTherapists in relation to the rise in professional complaints against them and the consequences this may have on their states of mind, as we see graphically in the suicides of nurses facing fitness to practice legal cases (Stacey, 2024). It is only when we accurately define the depth of the problem of mental health at work that we can shift the narrative to one that intentionally acknowledges the impact of uberization and jump off the neurolinguistic hamster wheel doomed to talk forever about workplace wellbeing.

Intentional realism

Let us intentionally engage with the realities of the trauma of work, and not deny it or underplay it in our relationships at work. We must push our trade unions and employers to campaign for the recognition of the real potential of work-related suicide and push for its articulation in employment law and health and safety regulatory structures. Ask your union branch to join campaigns that call for the recognition of work-related suicide and subscribe to those health and safety bodies that do serious work on this topic. Talk about bullying at work with colleagues and people you trust when it is safe enough for your experiences to be useful. If you work for an organization that has responsibility for the health and safety of workers that does not model its own standards, think about using your union membership to take a group action to challenge that.

The intention of AI-MHS

Platform research contends fairly consistently that online platforms have specific and intense occupational health safety and environmental (OHSE) risks, including intensification and fatigue, as well as psychosocial risks including burnout, isolation and algorithmic surveillance, and the implied grey- and blacklisting combined with dynamic pricing forming a potentially sick working environment (WIE, 2021, 2024). Health and safety are the Trojan horses of workplace organizing. In most parts of the world there are laws and inspection systems that exist, and a broad understanding that it is not acceptable for people to actually die at work. It means that in the realms of health and safety there exist advanced regulatory and inspection tools even in a neoliberal de-regulated country like the UK. Social science alerts us to the silencing and invisibility of the most expert and vulnerable frontline workers, and to the possibility that occupational risk is often greatly underrepresented in our workplace cultures. This omission distorts the data around work-related problems such as the extent of occupational trauma and mental illness (Smith et al, 2008), and misunderstanding what actions are likely to minimize harm.

Although positive health rights such as sick notes and sick pay are constantly being challenged and undermined, there is a rule of thumb that we can talk about health and safety in parts of the world where freedom of association cannot safely be said out loud. It is why so many trade unions do OHSE projects and take the election of a safety rep seriously, why so much EU money is paid towards it and why sometimes and in experienced political hands a stress management checklist can be a radical thing. Although there has always been a tension in the union debates about resilience and the uses and abuses of it (Cotton and Martinez Lucio, 2022), it is predominantly through the health and safety structures and surveys that we know quite how many people are burned out at work and that there might be an enforceable way to secure enough space to recover.

The big health problems, including mental health, unavoidably underline that risk flourishes on inequality which is mapped onto class, race, sex and geography and becomes automated within the process of digitalization and use of AI technologies (Eubanks, 2019). Even the high-profile institutional insider research on health inequalities by Michael Marmot recognizes that raising welfare benefits would be the easiest way to save lives (Stacey, 2024). The breathtaking attack on diversity and equality initiatives in the US (Agathocleous et al, 2024) signals that once policy is designed to allow us to look at inclusion without the responsibility of looking at who is actually getting excluded, the evidence base is at risk of being designed to support the political facts rather than find the scientific ones. Which is how it is that the US retail giant Costco became the poster child for responsible business in 2025 (D'Innocenzio, 2025).

The importance of diversity and inclusion being represented in workplace institutions, including scientific and political diversity, should not be underestimated because of the dominance of politically convenient scientific tribes in the digital health sector. If the politicization of science teaches us one thing, it is the necessity of the social sciences in understanding the social environment that shapes work, how it is done and who does it, and the intersection of environmental and embodied factors that influence our health and our safety. Working at this intersection requires taking a view beyond our own disciplines or industrial positions and engaging with mental health as a profoundly political project. It also requires genuine political leadership, which explains why some employers and trade unions, such as those in South Africa, are often way ahead in developing occupational responses to poor health. Far from the magic solutionism of wellbeing at work, OHSE recognizes that risk is an intrinsic part of ordinary occupational life and therefore something that has to be acknowledged and faced up to. This is the battleline for mental health at work, in fighting it out where the lines are drawn around safe and healthy platform practices, and a key point of leverage for UberTherapists who are organized into worker networks, and their health and safety reps plugging away on the mental health frontline.

Intentional AI-MHS

We need to expand our data and our thinking around AI-MHS that can establish the link between platform practices and the risks to the mental health of UberTherapists and the consumers of UberTherapy. We need to use existing worker organization models and ways of protecting worker data, of building case handling and representation capacities of therapists' networks and unions and even creating our own worker rights apps (Pinedo, 2021). We will need to build interdisciplinary and practical AI-MHS guidance for UberTherapy stakeholders on how to do it with the intentionality of protecting both consumers and therapists. If there was ever a training programme desperate to happen it is the AI-MHS programme for UberTherapists.

MuchBetterHelp

As any therapist will tell you, the world does not easily divide into good and bad people, but I am now going to say something snippy about Nick Clegg, who for me represents the friendly face of a dangerous middle ground in the new business of mental health. Sir Nick Clegg was the deputy prime minister of the UK's first coalition government between the Liberal Democrats and the Conservatives and for a while was the President of Global Affairs at Meta. A nice guy with liberal values overseeing the stress-testing of the Meta algorithms (Kleinman and Gerken, 2023) – open source and tech democracy – Nick ticks the transparency boxes by publishing Meta's data. In a debate on BBC Radio 4's *Today* programme in 2023 with Professor Dame Wendy Hall, co-Chair of the Government's AI Review, Wendy calls this the equivalent to 'giving people a template to build a nuclear bomb' (Milmo, 2023). Nick says this is hyperbole, having learned to dodge all manner of critical thought with an inbuilt confidence and associated unconscious bias of someone who exists in a parallel political universe. But in a way Nick was right that the real impact of AI is not in this moment of hyperbolic drama but it is determined in the details of its production. Whatever AI regulations and ethical certification are produced, unless they address the interlock between workers' and consumers' rights then AI will continue to evade its complex and dynamic relationship with our human rights.

As it stands now an estimated 2 per cent of mental health apps have research evidence to support their use (Goldberg et al, 2022) and it is in this unregulated system of digital therapy e-commerce that we are likely to see the greatest traction in bringing about regulation. It will be the regulation of therapy as e-commerce that will lead to the emergence of sustainability measurements and auditing for digital therapy and consumer rankings and ratings by the next generation of consumers. It is these consumers who will challenge the current solution-focused business model, as they take the greatest hit from side effects of a system of on-demand care, which is exactly as it should be. As we come to understand the UberTherapy business model we will become better placed to enter into the sustainability debates which hinge on whether we can design responsibility back into the therapy system. Consumer information will start to be mapped, and mental health apps will be ranked and rated on the basis of their data protection and privacy indexation.[7] Part of UberTherapy's consumer protections will be formed by the use of anonymous consumer surveys and AI technologies to monitor data that we genuinely consented to giving. We will see the production of mental health app AI secret shoppers to measure the harms and failings of UberTherapy, probably promoted through the future tribe of 'unrecovery' influencers. The question that will preoccupy the therapy sector will shortly become can we design a sustainable model for *RealTherapy*™ that stands to deliver much better help?

Decades of sustainability in practice in other sectors, and the current legal cases around digital therapy indicate the space is emerging for the creation of a series of Digital Therapy Kite Marks and fair trade labels. The regulatory and campaigning work would aim to establish a set of professional principles and protections specific to therapy that recognizes the interlock between practitioner and consumer protections and develops regulatory tools for AI-MHS on both sides of the therapeutic relationship. These responsibility tools would extend beyond online therapy platforms to AI technologies, including text-based services, chatbots, wellness and therapy apps that operate at the interface between the social and clinical.

Regulators already struggle with knowing which of the therapy apps are anything to do with them – using the language of 'software as medical device' (SaMD) or 'software in a medical device' (SiMD) (Nwosu et al, 2022) as a way of tapping into existing medical device regulation. The therapeutic risks and responsibilities of a piece of software are hard to pin down, which I guess is part of the point. We would struggle to say who is accountable for what happens after we download a therapy app, which explains why the big legal cases about therapy will take place in the advertising standards courts and why the new models of *RealTherapy*™ will be determined ultimately by who consumes it and who provides it. Already in the UK EAP sector we are seeing smaller, often domestic, companies arguing their competitive advantage of responsibility to potential employees by offering better hourly rates, stopping the practice of charging registration fees, offering direct contracts of employment, supervision and sick pay. Some are offering better hourly rates not linked to work intensification through the higher-rates-higher-caseload as we see in the UberTherapy business model. This is a particular moment in the trajectory of UberTherapy, because right now as qualified and experienced therapists walk away from the NHS or unwaged work in the third sector they get to look around at who offers them the best deal. It may be that the small responsible business model cannot ultimately compete with online therapy platforms, but right now they offer a competitive advantage in their differentiation that might lead to negotiated pay and better working conditions in the therapy sector.

Much of this shaping of *RealTherapy*™ will be done in other parts of the world by people from the digital tech world scarred by the rollercoaster of venture capital and offering their technical skills to monitor algorithmic accountability such as Frances Haugen's *Beyond the Screen*,[8] and Rumman Chowdhury and Jutta Williams' *Humane Intelligence*.[9] We have the emergence of ethical standards for mental health apps[10] and certification,[11] and we will see alternative AI futures (Buolamwini, 2023) most likely to develop the next generation of community-friendly AI technologies and business model design. Although the industry of responsibility is built on compromise, these initiatives can feed into debates about what next and, importantly, takes some of the progressive money off the streets and out of the hands of the broligarchy stuck in their unconscious desires to self-replicate. One of the attractions of creating alternative platforms is around freelancing – where self-employed therapists can bypass the inherent precarity through designing their own corporate administration and protection.[12] On the horizon are more radical models of business such as platform cooperatives,[13] and given the living memory of cooperatives and co-production within the mental health sector there is potentially enough expertise in the system to pull it off.

The attack on thinking that is taking place within mental health means that talking to journalists about digital therapy is essential, as it is often the place where the issues around consumer protection gain the most traction. Topics such as mental health and worker rights that used to clear a room now populate debates on social media, and for that reason journalists are often the best people to raise genuine public curiosity about the black box of UberTherapy. One of the conversations I was engaged in was with a team producing a documentary for Channel 4[14] about an online therapy platform. A team of young women, we talked a lot over several months about the programme and how to approach it without falling into the trap of blaming bad therapy on bad therapists rather than the more complex storyline about platformization, low wages, work intensification and burnout. As you would hope with the next generation of thinkers, they had their own ideas and made a programme about a company from the perspective of new therapy consumers, including influencers on social media. This inevitably runs the risk that bad therapists are regulated by public exposure but in the absence of institutions that can govern the digital therapy business I felt genuine hope watching the critical clarity of the young people going on the record about the damage that is being done.

Much of this is about finding a shared language and the difficult work of interdisciplinary collaboration that this requires. This is particularly true with consumers of therapy who do not yet look at the business model, nor do they know their therapist's wages and working conditions, so for them asking about the impact of caseloads and work intensification on containment is of limited value. For those of us who work in the deep, engagement about real therapy means learning to use the words of our customers in a way that opens up a discussion about their actual experiences rather than shuts it down. Otherwise the conversation about whether this is therapy or not is being carried out in parallel universes and, since we are the last therapists standing engaging with *RealTherapy*™, therapists must up a debate with consumers who understand profoundly the difference between what is advertised and what is being sold and between what you pay for and what you actually get.

Stop dancing for daddy

> Hair-n-Teeth was in a meeting the other day and realized that their entire career potentially represents a waste of time. Presenting ideas around AI-MHS for therapists in response to the burnout crisis, it became apparent that, on a deep level, nobody in the room wants to hear it. Halfway through a slide about critical action learning, as the words 'consciousness raising' came out of my mouth, I had the out-of-body experience of realizing in real time that I was no longer of any use, as my appeals to relationality were now part of a heritage industry called caring. Eyes looked down among the next generation of UberTherapy leadership unnerved by my hopelessly non-transactional professional status, thanks were given for my 'passionate' presentation and everyone backed away slowly as the disdain matrix rained down my screen in green binary lights. I consider this my Cary Cooper[15] moment when he shut the door to experiential groups and became the good-enough parental object of individual resilience. I had for the first time seen through the eyes of the transactional digital therapy sector what lies ahead. That being ancient and kind puts me at a disadvantage in the new business of mental health.

Throughout the writing of this book I found myself repeating a grotesque phrase 'dancing for daddy'. These are my cruel-but-safe words, used to trigger a repulsion to the part of me that has led to my making the same self-defeating mistake of attempting to be successful in a neoliberal paternalistic economic system that I am profoundly at odds with. It is a phrase that encourages me to stop believing in my own exceptionalism as my protection from the inevitable attack on my critical thinking. To stop my belief that somehow I am different.

Relationality, from a psychodynamic perspective, acknowledges that it is through our relationships with others that we survive and develop throughout our lives (Bowlby, 1969). Accepting this developmental 'fact of life' (Money-Kyrle, 1961) involves accepting that we are dependent on others while at the same time acknowledging the inherently insecure nature of the relationships we form with each other. It is despite this insecure nature of relationships that exchange and identifications between people are crucial and if there is a useful political generalization to be made it is that anything that stops you relating is a problem, in therapy and more broadly in society.

Many of us live in the middle age, in between our parents' generations where working-class people could 'do good' and our future of political and e-commercial transactions where younger generations are reluctantly set up to address our failures. Being in the middle age, which the majority of therapists are, I can see how we came to this point of denial (Cohen, 2000) that within our lifetime the crises of the economic and environmental systems have changed everything, including how we had to bury that knowledge. It is from this middle age position that we can see clearly the threat of disavowal of where we came from and the risks of forgetting our own stories, including the transgenerational fights to move beyond ideological and societal restrictions to really be ourselves. This denial exists in the AI therapy debates across different levels as we wade through misinformation and fakery, negation as a denial of facts including psychic ones, and disavowal where a knowing-not-knowing is enlisted to erase our memories and those of our professional parental objects.

In psychoanalytic thinking, a lot of room is given to the possibility that these forms of denial often function unconsciously in our cultures (Bell, 1999) and involve a splitting off of difficult feelings – a projection of what we cannot own and an idealization of its alternatives which we witness in the false-dawn technological solutionism in therapy. Noah's Arkism (Weintrobe, 2021) is the idea that in the face of hard realities we can fall into a self-sabotaging denial of the collective nature of our survival, believing we have a place on the boat by virtue of our excellence. For those of us who do not even think there is a boat, the prospect of solidarity towards those who see themselves as part of the chosen professional tribe, we are placed in an awful dilemma. How to allow for the deep work of psychodynamic practice which prioritizes listening to the psychic and emotional realities of others (Shedler, 2010) who are not like us and to convene these essential conversations across the ages. This is where we now stand, at the point of having to dig deep in having those political and complex conversations about UberTherapy.

I guess that if you have made it to the end of this book you will not mind me going radical-lite in my parting formulation of where next, the last power points on our journey towards doing something about UberTherapy.

- *Don't blame yourself*: Do not internalize the downgrade that is taking place on either side of the therapeutic relationship. Given the size of UberTherapy it could not possibly be your fault.
- *Don't keep calm and carry on*: Probably the most consistent piece of advice we receive when we're in trouble is 'don't get angry'. Well, that's a lot less useful than it sounds. In the current climate of uberization, it's very important that we accept that we will feel things about what's happening and that we don't roll out neurolinguistically programmed words every time something important needs to be looked at. We have to learn to tolerate each other's anger and distress and create a space where that can be expressed across generations without anyone feeling ashamed.
- *Don't be brilliant*: If it's true that UberTherapy is setting everyone up for failure then there are no professional successes to celebrate. Therapists, please stop believing you are exceptional. Once our professional egos have worked through the implications of that, the up side is that no longer do we have to respond to systemic failure by just working harder and more.
- *Don't go it alone*: If the entire history of worker organizing tells us anything, it's that we can all be split and divided unless we work at the everyday of our relationships. This includes the consumers of UberTherapy, their families, the lawyers taking on *TotalRecovery*, the worker networks and unions, the consumer watchdogs, the journalists involved in the long game of watching UberTherapy's next moves, the IT consultants who walked away from stupid. A common intention is emerging and if you see anyone hovering around it then grab them and don't let go.
- *Create safe and active spaces*: In order to talk openly about tackling UberTherapy we have to create and convene spaces that allow people to talk safely. It means doing the dog work of shutting down unmoderated chatrooms, showing self-discipline on social media, anonymizing groups and professional discussions to avoid blacklisting, setting better ground rules for debate including that it serves an actionable purpose. Only use methods that are likely to lead to an agreed way forward.

This final chapter proposes that, as therapists and consumers of therapy, we do anything that we think is going to build freedom of association and human rights, free speech and collective thinking, recognition of work-related suicide, and a usable model of AI-MHS. This can only be done if we elect ourselves to convene those coalitions that allow for a collective oversight and the co-designing of what digital therapies are offered and consumed. Whatever you do to realize this in your life is worth your time and worthy of you. Underpinning these lines of action is a way of working and a way of being that accepts that therapy is, at its best, an emancipatory project, so use it to raise your consciousness, fight the internal and external oppressors and confront reality as it is. It is this that allows us to reimagine and recreate a future therapy that does not shame either side of the therapeutic relationship by denying that human and worker rights are always and in all ways dependent on each other.

Notes

1. Executive Order US Government (2025) 'Ending Radical and Wasteful DEI Programmes and Preferencing'. Available from www.whitehouse.gov/presidential-actions/2025/01/ending-radical-and-wasteful-government-dei-programs-and-preferencing/ [Accessed 7 March 2025].
2. UNI Amazon Global Union Alliance, https://uniglobalunion.org/workers-rights/uni-amazon-global-union-alliance/
3. International Labour Conference 2025, www.ilo.org/digital-labour-platforms
4. Global Trade Union Alliance of Content Moderators, https://uniglobalunion.org/news/moderation-alliance/
5. International Lawyers Assisting Workers Network (ILAW), www.ilawnetwork.com/
6. Survival Surgeries, www.survivingwork.org/survival-guides-access/survival-surgeries
7. Mozilla Foundation, Data Futures Lab, https://foundation.mozilla.org/en/data-futures-lab/?utm_source=MoFo&utm_campaign=23-IP-Warmup-3&utm_medium=email&utm_term=en&utm_content=Buttont_Data_Futures_Lab
8. www.beyondthescreen.org/
9. www.humane-intelligence.org/
10. IEEE Standards Authority, https://standards.ieee.org/industry-connections/data-driven-tech-healthcare/
11. ORCHA, https://orchahealth.com/
12. Freelancers' Union, US https://freelancersunion.org/
13. Platform Cooperatives, https://platform.coop/
14. Channel 4 Untold, 'I Don't Trust My Therapist'. Available from www.youtube.com/watch?v=L9qNiFFB6HU [Accessed 7 March 2025].
15. iResilience, www.robertsoncooper.com/iresilience/

References

Abd-Alrazaq AA, Alajlani M, Abdallah Alalwan A, Bewick BM, Gardner P and Househ M (2019) An overview of the features of chatbots in mental health: a scoping review. *International Journal of Medical Informatics* 132: 103978.

Abendschön S and García-Albacete G (2021) It's a man's (online) world: personality traits and the gender gap in online political discussion. *Information, Communication & Society* 24(14): 2054–2074.

Ackroyd S and Thompson P (2022) *Organisational Misbehaviour* (second edition). Sage.

Adams R (2025) *The New Empire of AI: The Future of Global Inequality*. Polity.

Adams R and Walker P (2024) 'UK Science Minster apologises and pays damages after academic's libel action', *The Guardian*. Available from www.theguardian.com/politics/2024/mar/05/uk-science-minister-michelle-donelan-apologises-and-pays-damages-after-academics-libel-action [accessed 10 March 2025].

Adès R (2016) 'Winnicott: The 'good-enough mother' radio broadcasts', OUPblog. Available from https://blog.oup.com/2016/12/winnicott-radio-broadcasts/ [accessed 10 March 2025].

Agathocleous A, Conway K and Moore R (2024) *Trump on DEI and Anti-Discrimination Law: Rolling Back the Clock on Racial Justice*. American Civil Liberties Union.

Alaimo C and Kallinikos J (2021) Reality filters: managing by data: algorithmic categories and organizing. *Organization Studies* 42(9): 1385–1407.

Aldridge C and Corlett A (2023) *They Died Waiting: The Crisis in Mental Health – Stories of Loss and Stories of Hope*. Learning Social Worker Publications.

Allen R and Masters D (2024) *Artificial Intelligence (Regulation & Employment Rights) Bill*, TUC. Available from www.tuc.org.uk/research-analysis/reports/artificial-intelligence-regulation-and-employment-rights-bill [accessed 10 March 2025].

Alsugeir D, Adesuyan M, Talaulikar V, Wei L, Whittlesea C and Brauer R (2024) Common mental health diagnoses arising from or coinciding with menopausal transition and prescribing of SSRIs/SNRIs medications and other psychotropic medications. *Journal of Affective Disorders* 1(364): 259–265.

REFERENCES

American Hospital Association (2023) 'Amazon's One Medical ramps up its expansion in primary care'. Available from www.aha.org/aha-center-health-innovation-market-scan/2023-11-21-amazons-one-medical-ramps-its-expansion-primary-care [accessed 10 March 2025].

Armstrong D and Rustin M (2015) *Social Defences Against Anxiety: Explorations in a Paradigm*. Karnac.

Atkinson J and Collins P (2024) *Algorithmic Management and a New Generation of Rights at Work*. Institute of Employment Rights.

Atkinson P (2014) Lies, damned lies, and IAPT statistics. *Self & Society* 42(1–2): 18–19.

Aylward M and Locascio JJ (1995) Problems in the assessment of psychosomatic conditions in social security benefits and related commercial schemes. *Journal of Psychosomatic Research* 39(6): 755–765.

BACP (2022) 'SCoPEd Framework'. Available from www.bacp.co.uk/about-us/advancing-the-profession/scoped/scoped-framework/ [accessed 4 April 2025].

Baines D (2004) Caring for nothing: work organization and unwaged labour in social services. *Work, Employment and Society* 18(2): 267–295.

Bandinelli C and Bandinelli A (2021) What does the app want? A psychoanalytic interpretation of dating apps' libidinal economy. *Psychoanalysis, Culture & Society* 26(2): 181–198.

Bandinelli C and Gandini A (2022) Dating apps: the uncertainty of marketised love. *Cultural Sociology* 16(3): 423–441.

Barnes H (2023) *Time to Think: The Inside Story of the Collapse of the Tavistock's Gender Service for Children*. Swift Press.

Barnes S-A, Green A and de Hoyos M (2015) Crowdsourcing and work: individual factors and circumstances influencing employability. *New Technology, Work and Employment* 30(1): 16–31.

Bateson N (2022) New words to hold the invisible world of possibility: warm data, symmathesy and aphanipoiesis. *Unpsychology Issue* 8: 12–17.

Batha E (2024) 'Taylor Swift and deepfake porn: what's the law?', *Context*. Available from www.context.news/ai/taylor-swift-and-deepfake-porn-whats-the-law [accessed 7 March 2025].

Bazerman MH (2022) *Complicit: How We Enable the Unethical and How to Stop*. Princeton University Press.

BBC (2022) 'Crime Bill: MPs reject proposal to make misogyny a hate crime', *BBC News*. Available from www.bbc.com/news/uk-politics-60565216 [accessed 10 March 2025].

Bell D (1999) Introduction: Psychoanalysis, a Body of Knowledge of Mind and Human Culture. In D Bell (ed) *Psychoanalysis and Culture: A Kleinian Perspective*. Gerald Duckworth & Co. Ltd, pp 57–77.

Bendat M (2023) In Name Only? Mental Health Parity or Illusory Reform. In LM Michaels, T Wooldridge, N Burke and JR Muhr (eds) *Advancing Psychotherapy for the Next Generation: Humanizing Mental Health Policy and Practice*. Routledge, pp 57–77.

Bendell J (2023) 'Let's tell the moodsplainers they're wrong and then get back to work'. Available from https://jembendell.com/2023/08/05/lets-tell-the-moodsplainers-theyre-wrong-and-then-get-back-to-work/ [accessed 10 March 2025].

Beresford P, Nettle M and Perring R (2010) *Towards a Social Model of Madness and Distress? Exploring What Service Users Say*. Joseph Rowntree Foundation.

Berman Y and Horland T (2024) 'The impact of austerity on mortality and life expectancy'. International Inequalities Institute Working Paper 139. London School of Economics.

Beveridge J (2015) A Tangled Web: Internet Pornography, Sexual Addiction, and the Erosion of Attachment. In L Cundy (ed) *Love in the Age of the Internet: Attachment in the digital era*. Karnac, pp 31–52.

Bietti E (2022) Self-regulating platforms and antitrust justice. *Texas Law Review*, 101. http://dx.doi.org/10.2139/ssrn.4072084

Bonini T and Treré E (2024) *Algorithms of Resistance: The Everyday Fight against Platform Power*. MIT Press.

Booth P (2019a) 'England's NHS is embracing "big data". But who's really benefiting?', *OpenDemocracy*. Available from www.opendemocracy.net/en/ournhs/the-nhs-is-embracing-big-data-but-whos-really-benefiting/ [accessed 4 April 2025].

Booth R (2019b) 'Benefits system automation could plunge claimants deeper into poverty', *The Guardian*. Available from www.theguardian.com/technology/2019/oct/14/fears-rise-in-benefits-system-automation-could-plunge-claimants-deeper-into-poverty [accessed 10 March 2025].

Bossewitch J, Brown LXZ, Gooding P, Harris L, Horton J, Katterl S, et al (2021) *Digital Futures in Mind: Reflecting on Technological Experiments in Mental Health & Crisis Support*. University of Melbourne.

Bostoen, F (2018) Online platforms and pricing: adapting abuse of dominance assessments to the economic reality of free products. *Computer Law & Security Review* 35(3): 263–280.

Bowker GC (2010) Reflections from Geoffrey Bowker. *Science, Technology, and Human Values* 35(5): 579–580.

Bowlby J (1969) *Attachment and Loss: Volume 1 Attachment*. Basic Books.

Brave New Europe (2024) The Brussels Appeal: Proposal from the Forum on Alternatives to Uberisation. *BNE*. Available from https://braveneweurope.com/the-brussels-appeal-proposal-from-the-forum-on-alternatives-to-uberisation-21-22-february-2024#:~:text=Since%202019%2C%20gig%20economy%20workers,companies%20like%20Uber%20and%20Glovo [accessed 10 March 2025].

REFERENCES

Brown A (2022) *Dream Lovers: The Gamification of Relationships*. Pluto Press.

Brunnerová S, Ceccon D, Holubová B, Kahancová M, Lukáčová K and Medas G (2024) *New Technologies at the Workplace Collective Bargaining Practices on AI and Algorithmic Management in European Services Sector*. UNI Europa and FES.

Buolamwini J (2023) *Unmasking AI: My Mission to Protect What Is Human in a World of Machines*. Random House.

Burke N, Michaels LM and Muhr J (2023) Psychotherapy Action Network: Seeing beyond the Crossroads. In LM Michaels, T Wooldridge, N Burke and JR Muhr (eds) *Advancing Psychotherapy for the Next Generation: Humanizing Mental Health Policy and Practice*. Routledge, pp 8–16.

Burleigh A et al (eds) (2023) #saynotobullyinginmidwifery. #Saynoto bullyinginmidwifery Facebook Group.

Cadwallader C (2024) 'How to survive the broligarchy', *The Guardian*. Available from www.theguardian.com/commentisfree/2024/nov/17/how-to-survive-the-broligarchy-20-lessons-for-the-post-truth-world-donald-trump [accessed 10 March 2025].

Campbell D (2024) 'NHS across UK spends a "staggering" £10bn on temp staff', *The Guardian*. Available from www.theguardian.com/society/2024/jan/16/nhs-across-uk-spends-a-staggering-10bn-on-temporary-staff#:~:text=Ministers%20are%20facing%20calls%20to,than%20%C2%A310bn%20a%20year [accessed 10 March 2025].

Cappello M (ed) (2023) *Algorithmic Transparency and Accountability of Digital Services*. IRIS Special, European Audiovisual Observatory.

Carrigan M (2025) *Generative AI for Academics*. Sage.

Carter E and Whitworth A (2015) Creaming and parking in quasi-marketised welfare-to-work schemes: designed out of or designed in to the UK Work Programme? *Journal of Social Policy* 44(2): 277–296.

Case A and Deaton A (2020) *Deaths of Despair and the Future of Capitalism*. Princeton University Press.

Cass, H (2024) *Independent Review of Gender Identity Services for Children and Young People: Final Report*. Available from https://cass.independent-review.uk/home/publications/final-report/ [accessed 10 March 2025].

CBTWatch (2024a) 'BBC chooses to ignore Talking Therapies' 10% recovery rates', *Daily Mail*. Available from www.dailymail.co.uk/health/article-13231553/mental-health-sickness-work-therapy.html [accessed 7 March 2025].

CBTWatch (2024b) 'The Care Quality Commission and NHS Talking Therapies'. Available from www.cbtwatch.com/the-care-quality-commission-and-nhs-talking-therapies/ [accessed 29 April 2025].

CDEI (2019) *AI and Personal Insurance*. UK Government.

Chen L, Tong TW and Han STN (2022) Governance and design of digital platforms: a review and future research directions on a meta-organization. *Journal of Management* 48(1): 147–184.

CHPI (Centre for Health and the Public Interest) (2023) *The devil is in the detail: NHS England's contracts with the private hospital sector during COVID.* CHPI. Available from www.chpi.org.uk/reports/the-devil-is-in-the-detail [accessed 13May 2025].

Chun W (2021) *Discriminating Data: Correlation, Neighborhoods, and the New Politics of Recognition.* The MIT Press.

Clark DM, Canvin L, Green J, Layard R, Pilling S and Janecka M (2018) Transparency about the outcomes of mental health services (IAPT approach): an analysis of public data. *The Lancet* 391(10121): 679–686.

Clarke R (2018) 'Why Matt Hancock's promotion of Babylon worries doctors', *The BMJ Opinion*. Available from https://blogs.bmj.com/bmj/2018/12/04/rachel-clarke-why-matt-hancocks-promotion-of-babylon-worries-doctors/ [accessed 10 March 2025].

Clifford E (2020) *The War on Disabled People: Capitalism, Welfare and the Making of a Human Catastrophe.* Zed Books.

Cohen S (2000) *States of Denial: Knowing about Atrocities and Suffering.* Polity Press.

Colbert M (2023) 'A mysterious new addition to the Tufton Street clique', *BylineTimes*. Available from https://bylinetimes.com/2023/03/06/a-mysterious-new-addition-to-the-tufton-street-clique/ [accessed 10 March 2025].

Committee of Public Accounts (2014) *Contracting out Public Services to the Private Sector: Forty-seventh Report of Session 2013–14.* House of Commons. Available from https://publications.parliament.uk/pa/cm201314/cmselect/cmpubacc/777/777.pdf [accessed 10 March 2025].

Comunello F, Parisi L and Ieracitano F (2021) Negotiating gender scripts in mobile dating apps: between affordances, usage norms and practices. *Information, Communication & Society* 24(8): 1140–1156.

Coombe P (2019) The Northfield Experiments: a reappraisal 70 years on. *Group Analysis* 53(2): 162–176.

Cotton E, Kline R and Morton C (2013) Following Francis: reversing performance in the NHS from targets to teams. *People & Strategy*, 36(1): 63–65.

Collins J (2024) 'Minneapolis City Council votes to boost rideshare driver pay by veto proof majority', *MPR News*. Available from www.mprnews.org/story/2024/03/07/minneapolis-city-council-votes-to-boost-rideshare-driver-pay-by-veto-proof-majority [accessed 10 March 2025].

Conti-Cook C and Vogel E (2024) *MyCity, INC: A Case Against 'CompStat Urbanism'.* Surveillance Resistance Lab.

Cooiman F (2023) Veni vidi VC – the backend of the digital economy and its political making. *Review of International Political Economy* 30(1): 229–251.

Cooper A and Lousada J (2005) *Borderline Welfare: Feeling and Fear of Feeling in Modern Welfare*. Karnac Books.

Cotton E (2017) Constructing solidarities at work: relationality and the methods of emancipatory education. *Capital & Class* 42(2): 315–331.

Cotton E (2018) *Surviving Work in Healthcare: Helpful Stuff for People on the Frontline*. Taylor & Francis.

Cotton E (2019) The Industrial Relations of Mental Health. In C Jackson and R Rizq (eds) *The Industrialisation of Care: Counselling & Psychotherapy in a Neoliberal Age*. PCCS Books, pp 209–231.

Cotton E (2021) Wellbeing on the healthcare frontline: a safe laboratory for critical action learning. *Academy of Management Learning & Education* 20(4): 501–503.

Cotton E (2023) *The Financial Landscape of the Counselling & Psychotherapy Sector: Cost of Living Crisis*. Counsellors Together UK.

Cotton E and Royle T (2015) Transnational organising: a case study of contract workers in the Colombian mining industries. *British Journal of Industrial Relations* 52(4): 705–724.

Cotton E and Martinez Lucio M (2022) Trade Unions, Work and Resilience. In P Goulart, R Ramos and G Ferrittu (eds) *Globalization, Technology and Labour Resilience*. Palgrave Readers in Economics, pp 555–562.

Couldry N and Mejias U (2019) *The Costs of Connection: How Data is Colonizing Human Life and Appropriating it for Capitalism*. Stanford University Press.

Cox D (2024) '"They thought they were doing good but it made people worse": why mental health apps are under scrutiny', *The Observer*. Available from www.theguardian.com/society/2024/feb/04/they-thought-they-were-doing-good-but-it-made-people-worse-why-mental-health-apps-are-under-scrutiny [accessed 10 March 2025].

Cox J (2024) 'ID verification service for TikTok, Uber, X exposed driver licenses', *404 Media*. Available from www.404media.co/id-verification-service-for-tiktok-uber-x-exposed-driver-licenses-au10tix [accessed 10 March 2025].

Crawford K (2021) *Atlas of AI*. Yale University Press Books.

Croucher R and Cotton E (2011) *Global Unions Global Business: Global Union Federations and International Business* (second edition). Libri Publishing.

Crowther Z (2023) 'Falling mental health waiting lists "skewed" by drop-outs'. *Politics Home*. Available from www.politicshome.com/news/article/falling-nhs-mental-health-waiting-lists-skewed-drop-out-rates [accessed 4 April 2025].

Cundy L (2015) The Etherial M/other. In L Cundy (ed) *Love in the Age of the Internet: Attachment in the Digital Era*. Karnac, pp 169–176.

Dalal F (2018) *CBT: The Cognitive Behavioural Tsunami: Managerialism, Politics and the Corruptions of Science*. Routledge.

Das S (2023) 'UK mental health charities handed sensitive data to Facebook for targeted ads', *The Guardian*. Available from www.theguardian.com/society/2023/jun/03/uk-mental-health-charities-handed-sensitive-data-to-facebook-for-targeted-ads [accessed 10 March 2025].

Das S, Williams M and Ungoed-Thomas J (2023) 'Revealed: NHS England Chair fixed meeting for client of bank he advised', *The Guardian*. Available from www.theguardian.com/society/2023/feb/19/ex-nhs-england-chief-david-prior-teladoc-lazard [accessed 10 March 2025].

Davies R (2020) 'Betfred owners make millions from company treating gambling addicts', *The Guardian*. Available from www.theguardian.com/society/2020/jan/16/betfred-owners-make-millions-from-company-treating-gambling-addicts

Davis J (2021) *Sedated: How Modern Capitalism Created Our Mental Health Crisis*. Atlantic Books.

DHSC (Department of Health & Social Care) (2018) *The Future of Healthcare: Our Vision for Digital, Data and Technology in Health & Care*. UK Government.

Dicken P (2015) *Global Shift: Mapping the Changing Contours of the World Economy* (seventh edition). Guilford Press.

D'Innocenzio A (2025) 'Costco successfully defends diversity policies as other US companies scale theirs back', *The Associated Press*. Available from https://apnews.com/article/costco-shareholder-proposal-diversity-dei-0330f448741b35f2f788a36948ff3f95 [accessed 10 March 2025].

Doctorow C (2023) 'The "enshittification" of TikTok', *Wired*. Available from www.wired.com/story/tiktok-platforms-cory-doctorow/ [accessed 11 March 2025].

Drew P, Irvine A, Barkham M, Faija C, Gellatly J, Ardern K, et al (2021) Telephone delivery of psychological interventions: balancing protocol with patient-centred care. *Social Science & Medicine* 277: 113818.

Duguay S (2020) You can't use this app for that: exploring off-label use through an investigation of Tinder. *The Information Society* 36(1): 30–42.

Durnova A (2024) Psychosocial well-being, policies, and the emotional boundaries of home. *Critical Policy Studies*, 1–20. https://doi.org/10.1080/19460171.2024.2306237

DWP (Department for Work & Pensions) (2023) *Official Statistics: Universal Credit: 29 April 2013 to 13 July 2023*. UK Government.

Eilert N, Wogan R, Leen A and Richards D (2022) Internet-delivered interventions for depression and anxiety symptoms in children and young people: systematic review and meta-analysis. *JMIR Pediatrics and Parenting* 5(2): e33551. https://doi.org/10.2196/33551

REFERENCES

Elliott L (2024) 'Oasis fans are angry but dynamic pricing benefits consumers too', *The Guardian*. Available from www.theguardian.com/business/article/2024/sep/08/oasis-fans-angry-dynamic-pricing-benefits-consumers [accessed 10 March 2025].

Eltahawy A, Essig T, Myszkowski N and Trub L (2024) Can robots do therapy? Examining the efficacy of a CBT bot in comparison with other behavioral intervention technologies in alleviating mental health symptoms. *Computers in Human Behavior: Artificial Humans* 2(1). https://doi.org/10.1016/j.chbah.2023.100035.

EPRS (2023) 'Neurorights: Do our brains need to be protected by legislation?' Available from https://sciencemediahub.eu/2023/11/08/neurorights-do-our-brains-need-to-be-protected-by-legislation/ [accessed 8 May 2025].

EPRS (2024) The protection of mental privacy in the area of neuroscience: societal, legal and ethical challenges. STUDY Panel for the Future of Science and Technology. *European Parliamentary Research Service Scientific Foresight Unit (STOA) PE 757.807*.

Eubanks V (2019) *Automating Inequality: How High-Tech Tools Profile Police, and Punish the Poor*. Picador.

EU-OSHA (2024) 'Platform work: recent policy developments with OSH implications'. Available from https://oshwiki.osha.europa.eu/en/themes/platform-work-recent-policy-developments-osh-implications [accessed 4 April 2025].

European Commission (2018) 'A definition of AI: main capabilities and scientific disciplines', High-Level Expert Group on AI. Available from https://ec.europa.eu/futurium/en/system/files/ged/ai_hleg_definition_of_ai_18_december_1.pdf [accessed 10 March 2025].

European Commission (2021) 'The gender pay gap situation in the EU'. Available from https://commission.europa.eu/strategy-and-policy/policies/justice-and-fundamental-rights/gender-equality/equal-pay/gender-pay-gap-situation-eu_en [accessed 10 March 2025].

Evans C and Carlyle J (2021) *Outcome Measures and Evaluation in Counselling and Psychotherapy*. Sage Publications Ltd.

Farrar J and Cutillas S (2022) *Workers' Recommendations on the Draft EU Platform Work Directive*. Worker Info Exchange.

Federal Trade Commission (2023) 'FTC issues orders to eight companies seeking information on surveillance pricing'. Available from www.ftc.gov/news-events/news/press-releases/2024/07/ftc-issues-orders-eight-companies-seeking-information-surveillance-pricing [accessed 10 March 2025].

Federal Trade Commission (2024) 'BetterHelp customers will begin receiving notices about refunds related to a 2023 privacy settlement with FTC'. Available from www.ftc.gov/news-events/news/press-releases/2024/05/betterhelp-customers-will-begin-receiving-notices-about-refunds-related-2023-privacy-settlement-ftc [accessed 10 March 2025].

Ferrante M, Esposito LE and Stoeckel LE (2024) From palm to practice: prescription digital therapeutics for mental and brain health at the National Institutes of Health. *Frontiers in Psychiatry: Digital Mental Health* 15. https://doi.org/10.3389/fpsyt.2024.1433438

Financial Times (2021) 'The next big tech battle: Amazon's bet on healthcare'. Available from www.ft.com/content/fa7ff4c3-4694-4409-9ca6-bfadf3a53a62 [accessed 10 March 2025].

Fotaki M (2014) Can consumer choice replace trust in the National Health Service in England? Towards developing an affective psychosocial conception of trust in health care. *Sociology of Health and Illness* 36(8): 1276–1294.

Frazer-Caroll M (2023) *Mad World: The Politics of Mental Health*. Pluto Press.

Freire P (1970) *Pedagogy of the Oppressed*. Continuum Books.

Freud D (2021) *Clashing Agendas: Inside the Welfare Trap*. Nine Elms Books.

Freud S (1905) Three Essays on the Theory of Sexuality. In *Standard Edition of the Complete Psychological Works of Sigmund Freud*, 7: 123–245.

Friedli L and Stearn R (2015) Positive affect as coercive strategy: conditionality, activation and the role of psychology in UK government workfare programmes. *Medical Humanities* 41: 40–47.

Fromm E (1976) *To Have or to Be?* Bloomsbury.

Future Care Capital (2024) 'Outsourcing mental health services is proving costly for the NHS'. Available from https://futurecarecapital.org.uk/latest/outsourcing-nhs-mental-health-services-proving-costly/#:~:text=NHS%20mental%20health%20trusts%20are,ago%2C%20the%20paper%20has%20calculated [accessed 10 March 2025].

Ganesh, A (2024) Predatory pricing in platform markets: a modified test for firms within the scope of Article 3 of the DMA and super-dominant platform firms under Article 102 TFEU. *European Competition Journal*, 1–36. https://doi.org/10.1080/17441056.2024.2428032

Garofalo L (2024) *Doing the Work: Therapeutic Labor, Teletherapy and the Platformization of Mental Health Care*, Data & Society. Available from https://datasociety.net/wp-content/uploads/2024/05/DS_Doing_the_Work.pdf [accessed 1 May 2025].

Giustini D (2022) 'Gender inequalities and invisible work in the platform economy', *Women's Budget Group*. Available from www.wbg.org.uk/article/gender-inequality-and-invisible-work-in-the-platform-economy [accessed 10 March 2025].

Glasser M (1992) Problems in the psychoanalysis of certain narcissistic disorders. *International Journal of Psychoanalysis* 73: 493–503.

Goldberg SB, Lam SU, Simonsson O, Torous J and Sun S (2022) Mobile phone-based interventions for mental health: a systematic meta-review of 14 meta-analyses of randomized controlled trials. *PLOS Digital Health* 1(1): e0000002. https://doi.org/10.1371/journal.pdig.0000002

REFERENCES

Goodman DM (2015) The McDonaldization of psychotherapy: processed foods, processed therapies, and economic class. *Theory & Psychology* 26(1): 77–95.

Gumbrell-McCormick R and Hyman R (2013) *Trade Unions in Western Europe: Hard Times, Hard Choices*. Oxford University Press.

Gyimah M, Azad Z, Begum S, Kapoor A, Ville L, Henderson A and Dey M (2022) *Broken Ladders: The Myth of Meritocracy for Women of Colour in the Workplace*. Fawcett Society and Runnymede Trust.

Hadar-Shoval D, Elyoseph Z and Maya Lvovsky (2023) The plasticity of ChatGPT's mentalizing abilities: personalization for personality structures. *Frontiers in Psychiatry: Digital Mental Health* 14. https://doi.org/10.3389/fpsyt.2023.1234397

Haidt J (2025) *The Anxious Generation: How the Great Rewiring of Childhood Is Causing an Epidemic of Mental Illness*. Penguin.

Halton W (2015) Obsessional–Punitive Defences in Care Systems: Menzies Lyth Revisited. In D Armstrong and M Rustin (eds) *Social Defences Against Anxiety: Explorations in a Paradigm*. Karnac, pp 27–38.

Harte A (2024) '"Eavesdropping" workplace help line has accreditation suspended', *BBC*. Available from www.bbc.com/news/articles/c89w2vjyy4go [accessed 10 March 2025].

Harte A and Rule E (2024) 'Workplace mental health service firm faces investigation', *BBC*. Available from www.bbc.com/news/uk-68537252 [accessed 10 March 2025].

Hassel A and Hertie FS (2022) The platform effect: how Amazon changed work in logistics in Germany, the United States and the United Kingdom. *European Journal of Industrial Relations* 28(3): 363–382.

Hauben H (ed), Lenaerts K and Waeyaert W (2020) *The platform economy and precarious work*. Publication for the committee on Employment and Social Affairs. Policy Department for Economic, Scientific and Quality of Life Policies, European Parliament.

Hayes C (2025) *The Sirens' Call: How Attention Became the World's Most Endangered Resource*. Scribe.

Haynes T (2024) 'The Mickey Mouse degrees that could damage your career prospects', *The Telegraph*. Available from www.telegraph.co.uk/money/consumer-affairs/worst-university-degrees-damage-career-prospects/ [accessed 10 March 2025].

Hinshelwood RD (1989) *A Dictionary of Kleinian Thought*. Free Association Books.

Hinshelwood RD (1991) *A Dictionary of Kleinian Thought* (second edition). Free Association Books.

Hinshelwood RD (2024) *Unconscious Politics: Alienation, Social Science and Psychoanalysis*. Karnac.

Hodgson C (2024) 'Uber chief unlocks $136mn in shares after beating $120bn valuation target', *Financial Times*. Available from www.ft.com/content/6a59da30-a7c7-4b65-a9af-b1195262ad33 [accessed 10 March 2025].

Holgate J and Page J (2025) *Change Makers: Radical Strategies for Social Movement Organising*. Policy Press.

Hood L, Balling R and Auffray C (2012) Revolutionizing medicine in the 21st century through systems approaches. *Biotechnology Journal* 7(8): 992–1001.

Huber L, Pierce C and Lindtner S (2022) An approximation of freedom: on-demand therapy and the feminization of labor. *Proceedings of the ACM Human-Computer Interaction* 6: 275. https://doi.org/10.1145/3555166

Hutter M (2012) One Decade of Universal Artificial Intelligence. In P Wang and B Goertzel (eds) *Theoretical Foundations of Artificial General Intelligence*. Atlantis Thinking Machines, vol 4. Atlantis Press, pp 68–88.

Huws U (2015) *The Future of Work: Crowdsourcing*. European Agency for Safety and Health at Work.

Huws U (2024) Algorithmic violence. *Work Organisation, Labour & Globalisation* 18(1): 97–122.

Huws U and Spencer N (eds) (2022) *Seven Ways Platform Workers Are Fighting Back*. TUC.

Huws U, Spencer N and Coates M (2019) *The Platformisation of Work in Europe: Highlights from Research in 13 European Countries*. Foundation for European Progressive Studies.

Huws U et al (2024) Algorithmic violence. *Work Organisation, Labour & Globalisation* 18(1): 97–122.

Irvine A and Rose N (2022) How does precarious employment affect mental health? A scoping review and thematic synthesis of qualitative evidence from Western economies. *Work, Employment and Society* 38(2). https://doi.org/10.1177/09500170221128698

Islam G, Pillet J-C, Navazhylava K and Barros M (2021) High-performance connections: digital holism and communicative capitalism at HappyAppy. *Organization* 30(5): 1046–1073.

Jacques E (1951) *The Changing Culture of a Factory: A Study of Authority and Participation in an Industrial Setting*. Tavistock.

Jaffe S (2021) *Work Won't Love You Back: How Devotion to Our Jobs Keeps Us Exploited, Exhausted and Alone*. Hurst & Company.

Kale S (2024) 'The life and tragic death of John Balson: how a true crime producer documented his own rising horror', *The Guardian*. Available from www.theguardian.com/tv-and-radio/article/2024/aug/14/the-life-and-tragic-death-of-john-balson-how-a-true-producer-documented-his-own-rising-horror [accessed 10 March 2025].

Kalleberg K (2018) Job insecurity and well-being in rich democracies. *The Economic and Social Review* 49(3): 241–258.

REFERENCES

Kassem S (2024) *Work and alienation in the platform economy: Amazon and the power of organization*. Bristol University Press.

Khan M, Williams J, Williams P and Mayes R (2024) Caring in the gig economy: a relational perspective of decent work. *Work, Employment and Society* 38(4): 1107–1125.

King H (2022) 'COVID opens new door for Amazon health care ambition', *Axios*. Available from www.axios.com/2022/07/21/amazon-acquisition-one-medical-covid-healthcare [accessed 10 March 2025].

Kislev E (2022) *Relationships 5.0: How AI, VR, and Robots Will Reshape Our Emotional Lives*. Oxford University Press.

Klair A (2023) 'BME women far more likely to be on zero-hours contracts', *itvNEWS*. Available from www.itv.com/news/2024-04-26/bme-women-twice-as-likely-to-be-on-zero-hours-contracts-as-white-men [accessed 10 March 2025].

Klein N (2023) TikTok is not your doctor: reprioritizing consumer protection in pharmaceutical advertisement regulation. *Belmont Law Review* 11(2): Article 6.

Kleinmen Z and Gerken T (2023) 'Nick Clegg: AI language systems are "quite stupid"', *BBC*. Available from www.bbc.com/news/technology-66238004 [accessed 7 March 2025].

Kline R and Lewis D (2018) The price of fear: estimating the financial cost of bullying and harassment to the NHS in England. *Public Money & Management* 39(3): 166–174.

Kollewe J (2024) '"No one's being honest about it": how NHS crisis forces patients to go private', *The Guardian*. Available from www.theguardian.com/business/2024/apr/28/no-ones-being-honest-about-it-how-nhs-crisis-forces-patients-to-go-private [accessed 1 May 2025].

Konzelmann SJ (2019) *Austerity*. Polity Press.

Korczynski M (2003) Communities of coping: collective emotional labour in service work. *Korczynski Organization* 10(1): 55–75.

Kroenke K, Spitzer RL and Williams JB (2001) The PHQ-9: validity of a brief depression severity measure. *Journal of General International Medicine* 16(9): 606–613.

Krüger S (2024) *Formative Media: Psychoanalysis and Digital Media Platforms*. Routledge.

Krüger S and Spilde AC (2020) Judging books by their covers: Tinder interface, usage and sociocultural implications. *Information, Communication & Society* 23(10): 1395–1410.

Kurzweil R (2005) *The Singularity Is Near: When Humans Transcend Biology*. Penguin Books.

Kuzminskaite E and Childhood Trauma Meta-Analysis Study Group (2022) Treatment efficacy and effectiveness in adults with major depressive disorder and childhood trauma history: a systematic review and meta-analysis. *The Lancet Psychiatry* 9(11): 860–873.

Lanxon N (2019) 'Alphabet's DeepMind takes on billion dollar debt and loses $572 million', *Bloomberg*. Available from www.bloomberg.com/news/articles/2019-08-07/alphabet-s-deepmind-takes-on-billion-dollar-debt-as-loss-spirals?leadSource=uverify%20wall [accessed 1 May 2025].

Larson C (2024) 'BetterHelp refunded customers $93M in 2023', *Behavioural Health Business*. Available from https://bhbusiness.com/2024/03/01/betterhelp-refunded-customers-93m-in-2023/ [accessed 10 March 2025].

Law Commission (2021) *Hate Crime Laws: Final Report*. Law Com No402.

Layard R, Bell S, Clark DM, Knapp M, Meacher M and Priebe S (2006) *The Depression Report: A New Deal for Depression and Anxiety Disorders*. London School of Economics.

Layton L (2020) *Toward a Social Psychoanalysis: Culture, Character, and Normative Unconscious Processes*. Routledge.

Lazar S (2023) The Cost-effectiveness of Psychodynamic Therapy: The Obstacles, the Law, and a Landmark Lawsuit. In LM Michaels, T Wooldridge, N Burke and JR Muhr (eds) *Advancing Psychotherapy for the Next Generation: Humanizing Mental Health Policy and Practice*. Routledge, pp 38–56.

Leichsenring F and Steinert C (2017) Is cognitive behavioral therapy the gold standard for psychotherapy? The need for plurality in treatment and research. *JAMA* 318(14): 1323–1324.

Levine A (2022) 'Suicide hotline shares data with for-profit spinoff, raising ethical questions', *Politico*. Available from www.politico.com/news/2022/01/28/suicide-hotline-silicon-valley-privacy-debates-00002617 [accessed 10 March 2025].

Levy K (2023) *Data Driven: Truckers, Technology, and the New Workplace Surveillance*. Princeton University Press.

Liang Y, Aroles J and Brandl B (2022) Charting platform capitalism: definitions, concepts and ideologies. *New Technology, Work and Employment* 37: 308–327.

Loukissas YA (2019) *All Data Are Local: Thinking Critically in a Data Driven Society*. The MIT Press.

Lynton L (2020) *Toward a Social Psychoanalysis: Culture, Character, and Normative Unconscious Processes*. Routledge.

Macdonald F, Bentham E, Malone J (2018) Wage theft, underpayment and unpaid work in marketised social care. *The Economic and Labour Relations Review* 29(1): 80–96.

MacKay AJ and Weinstein SN (2021) 'Dynamic pricing algorithms'. Harvard Business Review Working Paper 22–050.

REFERENCES

Macy J and Johnstone C (2022) *Active Hope (Revised): How to Face the Mess We're in with Unexpected Resilience and Creative Power*. New World Library.

Magill R (2024) *Work-related Suicide: Examining the Role of Work Factors in Suicide*. Worksafe: New Zealand Government.

Marsh S and Garcia CA (2024) 'Private equity groups collecting millions to run UK government-funded sexual assault referral centres', *The Guardian*. Available from www.theguardian.com/business/2024/mar/13/uk-private-equity-firms-sexual-assault-referral-centres?CMP=share_btn_url [accessed 10 March 2025].

Marshall, B (2022) *Data Conscience: Algorithmic Siege on Our Humanity*. Wiley.

Martin C, Iqbal Z, Airey ND and Marks L (2022) Improving Access to Psychological Therapies (IAPT) has potential but is not sufficient: how can it better meet the range of primary care mental health needs? *British Journal of Clinical Psychology* 61(1): 157–174.

Masterson L and Cetera M (2024) 'What's the difference between PPO and HMO health insurance?', *Forbes*. Available from www.forbes.com/advisor/health-insurance/hmo-vs-ppo/ [accessed 10 March 2025].

Mattioli D (2024) *The Everything War: Amazon's Ruthless Quest to Own the World and Remake Corporate Power*. Transworld Publishers.

McCrickard R (2024) The Mental Health Therapist Shortage Starts at Graduation: How to Help the 57% that Never Attain Licensure. *Motivo*. Available from https://4776111.fs1.hubspotusercontent-na1.net/hubfs/4776111/Motivo_Whitepaper.pdf [accessed 4 April 2025].

McCroskey K (2024) 'Teladoc secretly shares telehealth website user's data with Facebook Class Action Claims', *Newswire*. Available from www.classaction.org/news/teladoc-secretly-shares-telehealth-website-users-data-with-facebook-class-action-claims [accessed 10 March 2025].

McKelvey F and Hunt R (2019) Discoverability: toward a definition of content discovery through platforms. *Social Media & Society* 5(1). https://doi.org/10.1177/2056305118819188

McKiernan J (2024) 'Secret files reveal fears over future of NHS IT giant', *BBC*. Available from www.bbc.com/news/articles/cp33evkxz5go [accessed 10 March 2025].

McKinsey (2023) *The State of AI in 2023: Generative AI's Breakout Year*. McKinsey.

McQuillan D (2022) *Resisting AI: An Anti-fascist Approach to Artificial Intelligence*. Bristol University Press.

McShane J (2022) 'Timnit Gebru is part of a wave of Black women working to change AI', *NBC News*. Available from www.nbcnews.com/news/nbcblk/timnit-gebru-part-wave-black-women-working-change-ai-rcna13339 MNC News [accessed 10 March 2025].

Meltzer DW (1967) *The Psychoanalytic Process*. Heinemann.

MHRA (Medicines & Healthcare Products Regulatory Agency) (2023) 'Aripiprazole (Abilify): reminder on known risk of gambling disorder', *GOV.UK*. Available from www.gov.uk/government/news/aripiprazole-abilify-reminder-on-known-risk-of-gambling-disorder [accessed 10 March 2025].

Michaels LM, Muhr J and Burke N (2023) Stepping toward the Future: PsiAN's Vision. In LM Michaels, T Wooldridge, N Burke and JR Muhr (eds) *Advancing Psychotherapy for the Next Generation: Humanizing Mental Health Policy and Practice*. Routledge, pp 298–302.

Mills C (2014) *Decolonizing Global Mental Health: The Psychiatrization of the Majority World*. Routledge.

Milmo D (2023) 'Why is Meta releasing open-source AI model and are there any risks?', *The Guardian*. Available from www.theguardian.com/technology/2023/jul/19/why-is-meta-releasing-llama-2-open-source-ai-model-mark-zuckerberg [accessed on 13 March 2025].

Milmo D (2025) 'Kate Bush and Damon Albarn among 1,000 artists on silent AI protest album', *The Guardian*. Available from www.theguardian.com/technology/2025/feb/25/kate-bush-damon-albarn-1000-artists-silent-ai-protest-album-copyright [accessed 10 March 2025].

Moncrieff J, Cooper RE, Stockmann T, Amendola S, Hengartner MP and Horowitz MA (2023) The serotonin theory of depression: a systematic umbrella review of the evidence. *Molecular Psychiatry* 28(8): 3243–3256.

Money-Kyrle R (1961) *Man's Picture of His World and Three Papers*. Karnac.

Morgan D (ed) (2020) *The Deeper Cut: Further Explorations of the Unconscious in Social and Political Life*. Phoenix Publishing House.

Morgan D and Ruszczynski S (eds) (2007) *Lectures on Violence, Perversion and Delinquency*. Karnac Books.

Morgan J (2024) 'Donelan apologises for sharing UKRI letter online after payout', *Times Higher Education*. Available from www.timeshighereducation.com/news/donelan-apologises-tweeting-letter-ukri-0 [accessed 10 March 2025].

Morris, JW and Murray, S (eds) (2018) *Appified: Culture in the Age of Apps*. University of Michigan Press.

Mozilla Foundation (2024) 'Accelerating progress toward trustworthy AI', *Mozilla Foundation*. Available from https://assets.mofoprod.net/network/documents/Mozilla_Accelerating_Progress_Toward_Trustworthy_AI_v3.pdf [accessed 10 March 2025].

Mundell E (2024) 'Biden administration issues rules making mental health care more accessible', *US News*. Available from www.usnews.com/news/health-news/articles/2024-09-09/biden-administration-issues-rules-making-mental-health-care-more-accessible [accessed 10 March 2025].

REFERENCES

Murgia M (2022) 'Palantir tech to help out NHS elective care backlog', *Financial Times*. Available from www.ft.com/content/c1e9f47c-8b20-47d4-9f52-1c16f4ceba29 [accessed 10 March 2025].

Myers E (2024) 'Don't turn us into social security cops, banks tell UK government', *Politico*. Available from www.politico.eu/article/rishi-sunak-social-security-cops-uk-government/ [accessed 10 March 2025].

National Union of Healthcare Workers (2025) 'Tentative agreement reached to end Kaiser mental health strike'. Available from https://home.nuhw.org/2025/05/05/tentative-agreement-reached-to-end-kaiser-mental-health-strike/ [accessed 8 May 2025].

New York State Attorney General (2023) 'Attorney General James secures $328 million from Uber and Lyft for taking earnings from drivers'. Available from https://ag.ny.gov/press-release/2023/attorney-general-james-secures-328-million-uber-and-lyft-taking-earnings-drivers [accessed 10 March 2025].

Novelli C, Hacker P, Morley J, Trondal J and Floridi L (2024) A robust governance for the AI Act: AI Office, AI Board, Scientific Panel, and national authorities (May 5, 2024). *European Journal of Risk Regulation*. https://doi.org/10.2139/ssrn.4817755

NSUN (National Survivor User Network) (2024) *The Language of the Mental Health Lived Experience Landscape*. NSUN.

Nwosu A, Boardman S, Husain MM and Doraiswamy PM (2022) Digital therapeutics for mental health: is attrition the Achilles heel? *Frontiers in Psychiatry* 13: 900615. https://doi.org/10.3389/fpsyt.2022.900615

Oakes O (2023) 'Why Gymbox's fake ad crossed a line', *The Media Leader*. Available from https://the-media-leader.com/why-gymboxs-fake-ad-crossed-a-line [accessed 10 March 2025].

Obholzer A and Zagier Roberts V (2019) *The Unconscious at Work: A Tavistock Approach to Making Sense of Organizational Life* (second edition). Routledge.

ODM (Observatoire des Multinationales) (2022) *Uber Files 2 in Brussels Driving EU Lobbying Study*. ODM.

O'Dwyer ST, Sansom A, Mars B, Reakes L, Andrewartha C, Melluish J and Janssens A (2024) Suicidal thoughts and behaviors in parents caring for children with disabilities and long-term illnesses. *Archives of Suicide Research*, 1–18. https://doi.org/10.1080/13811118.2024.2363230

OHID (Office for Health Improvement & Disparities) (2025) *Official Statistics. Statistical Report: Near to Real-time Suspected Suicide Surveillance (nRTSSS) for England for the 15 Months to October 2024*. UK Government.

Oksman O (2016) 'US firms look to capitalise as NHS becomes increasingly privatized', *The Guardian*. Available from www.theguardian.com/society/2016/feb/08/us-firms-look-to-capitalise-as-nhs-becomes-increasingly-privatised [accessed 10 March 2025].

O'Neil C (2022) *The Shame Machine: Who Profits in the New Age of Humiliation.* Penguin.

Pan W, Deng F, Wang X, Hang B, Zhou W and Zhu T (2023) Exploring the ability of vocal biomarkers in distinguishing depression from bipolar disorder, schizophrenia, and healthy controls. *Frontiers in Psychiatry: Digital Mental Health* 14. https://doi.org/10.3389/fpsyt.2023.1079448

Pardo-Guerra JP (2022) *The Quantified Scholar: How Research Evaluations Transformed the British Social Sciences.* Columbia University Press.

Park P (1999) People, knowledge, and change in participatory research. *Management Learning* 30(2): 141–157.

Partners for Counselling & Psychotherapy (2022) 'Locked gateways – the final iteration of SCoPEd'. Available from www.partnersforcounselling andpsychotherapy.co.uk/pcp-response-to-january-2022-iteration-of-the-scoped-framework/ [accessed 4 April 2025].

Philipson IJ (1993) *On the Shoulders of Women: The Feminization of Psychotherapy.* Guilford Press.

Pinedo E (2021) 'Spanish unions to get access to app algorithms to monitor workers' rights', *Reuters*. Available from www.reuters.com/article/business/spanish-unions-to-get-access-to-app-algorithms-to-monitor-workers-rights-idUSL8N2L94DL [accessed 10 March 2025].

Pope R (2024) *Platformland: An Anatomy of Next-generation Public Services.* London Publishing Partnership.

Pring J (2024a) *The Department: How a Violent Government Bureaucracy Killed Hundreds and Hid the Evidence.* Pluto Press.

Pring J (2024b) 'New DWP bank "snooping powers" would "treat disabled people like criminals"', *Disability News Service.* Available from www.disabi litynewsservice.com/new-dwp-bank-snooping-powers-would-treat-disab led-people-like-criminals/#:~:text=Under%20current%20rules%2C%20 DWP%20can,having%20secured%20nearly%2080%2C000%20signatures [accessed 10 March 2025].

Proctor G and Hayes C (2017) Counselling for depression: a response to counselling education in the twenty-first century. Ethical conflicts for a counselling approach operating within a medicalised bureaucratic health service. *British Journal of Guidance & Counselling* 45(4): 417–426.

PSA (Professional Standards Authority) (2021) Public Briefing Paper: Concerns about proposed regulatory changes to the ethos of the voluntary Accredited Registers Programme and impact on the accessibility of psychotherapy and counselling and service user choice in the UK'. Available from https://web.archive.org/web/20210905161816/https://ahpp.org.uk/wp-content/uploads/2021/08/BRIEFING-PAPER-PSA-Changes-V3-Aug-2021.pdf [accessed 10 March 2025].

REFERENCES

Pulignano V, Grimshaw D, Domecka M and Vermeerbergen L (2024) Why does unpaid labour vary among digital labour platforms? Exploring socio-technical platform regimes of worker autonomy. *Human Relations* 77(9): 1243–1271.

Pybus J and Coté M (2022) Did you give permission? Datafication in the mobile ecosystem. *Information, Communication & Society* 25(11): 1650–1668.

Pyper D and Tyler-Todd J (2024) Prohibiting Conversion Therapy. *House of Commons Library Research Briefing*, 22 February 2024.

Rahman KS and Thelen K (2019) The rise of the platform business model and the transformation of twenty-first-century capitalism. *Politics & Society* 47(2): 177–204.

Rainone S and Aloisi A (2024) The EU Platform Work Directive: what's new, what's missing, what's next? *ETUI Policy Brief*.

Ralston W (2021) 'They told their therapists everything: hackers leaked it all', *Wired*. Available from www.wired.com/story/vastaamo-psychotherapy-patients-hack-data-breach/ [accessed 10 March 2025].

Ratner A (2024) 'Oedipus returns: everything you wanted to know about MILFs but were too uncomfortable to ask', *The American Psychoanalyst*. Available from https://tapmagazine.org/all-articles/oedipus-returns [accessed 10 March 2025].

Renton D (2021) *No Free Speech for Fascists: The Ideological Capture of Free Speech*. Routledge.

Rizq R (2011) IAPT, anxiety & envy: a psychoanalytic view of NHS primary care mental health services. *British Journal of Psychotherapy* 27(1): 37–55.

Rizq R (2012) The ghost in the machine: IAPT and organizational melancholia. *British Journal of Psychotherapy* 28(3): 319–335.

Rizq R (2013) States of abjection. *Organization Studies* 34(9): 1277–1297.

Rizq R (2014) Perversion, neoliberalism and therapy: the audit culture in mental health services. *Psychoanalysis, Culture & Society* 19: 209–218.

Rosa SK (2023) *Radical Intimacy*. Pluto Press.

Roxby P and Loader V (2024) 'NHS 111 offers new mental health service', *BBC News*. Available from www.bbc.com/news/articles/c20715d6yvxo [accessed 10 March 2025].

Rubery J (2015) Austerity and the future for gender equality in Europe. *ILR Review* 68(4): 715–741.

Rufo Y (2024) 'NHS nurse Amy Gallagher is SDP's London mayoral candidate', *BBC News*. Available from www.bbc.com/news/uk-england-london-67871119 [accessed 10 March 2025].

Ruiz R (2024) 'California paid millions to access a mental health app. It wasn't safe for users', *Mashable*. Available from https://mashable.com/article/7-cups-tech-suite-california-deal [accessed 10 March 2025].

Rustin M (2013) How is Climate Change an Issue for Psychoanalysis? In S Weintrobe (ed) (2013) *Engaging with Climate Change: Psychoanalytic and Interdisciplinary Perspectives*. Routledge, pp 170–185.

Samuels A (2015) *The Political Psyche*. Routledge.

Samuels A and Veale D (2009) Improving access to psychological therapies: for and against. *Psychodynamic Practice* 15(1): 41–56.

Schnitzer A and Hemmeke K (2019) 'Driven to resistance: taxi driver suicides in Korea and the US', *International Strategy Centre*. Available from www.goisc.org/englishblog/2019/5/7/driven-to-resistance-taxi-driver-suicides-in-korea-and-the-us [accessed 10 March 2025].

Schram SF and Silverman B (2012) The end of social work: neoliberalizing social policy implementation. *Critical Policy Studies* 6(2): 128–145.

Scott MJ (2018) Improving Access to Psychological Therapies (IAPT): the need for radical reform. *Journal of Health Psychology* 23(9): 1136–1147.

Scott MJ (2021) Ensuring that the Improving Access to Psychological Therapies (IAPT) programme does what it says on the tin. *British Journal of Clinical Psychology* 60: 38–41.

Scott MJ, Crawford JS, Geraghty KJ and Marks DF (2021) The 'medically unexplained symptoms' syndrome concept and the cognitive-behavioural treatment model. *Journal of Health Psychology* 27(1): 3–8.

Sharland H (2024) 'Trivialising Long Covid? Scientists and media covering ME/CFS in Australia wrote the playbook', *The Canary*. Available from www.thecanary.co/global/2024/03/27/trivialising-long-covid-scientists-and-media-covering-me-cfs-in-australia-wrote-the-playbook/ [accessed 10 March 2025].

Shedler J (2010) The efficacy of psychodynamic psychotherapy. *American Psychologist* 65(2): 98–109.

Shestakofsky B (2024) *Behind the Startup: How Venture Capital Shapes Work, Innovation and Inequality*. University of California Press.

Shrier A (2024) *Bad Therapy: Why the Kids Aren't Growing Up*. Swift Press.

Simister K (2023) 'Babylon Health rescue merger collapses', *UKTN*. Available from www.uktech.news/medtech/babylon-rescue-merger-collapses-20230808#:~:text=On%20the%20same%20day%20as,purpose%20acquisition%20company%2C%20or%20SPAC [accessed 10 March 2025].

Simms P (2024) *Reimagining Big Pharma with Elon Musk as CEO*. Impatient.

Smith C, Valsecchi R, Mueller F and Gabe J (2008) Knowledge and the discourse of labour process transformation: nurses and the case of NHS Direct for England. *Work, Employment and Society* 22(4): 581–599.

Socialist Health Association (2024) 'Replacing Qualified Doctors: A threat to patient safety'. Available from https://sochealth.co.uk/2024/09/03/labour-conference-motion-replacing-qualified-doctors/ [accessed 10 March 2025].

Speed E and Mannion R (2020) Populism and health policy: three international case studies of right-wing populist policy frames. *Sociology of Health & Illness* 42(8): 1967–1981.

Spitzer RL, Kroenke K, Williams JBW and Löwe B (2006) A brief measure for assessing Generalized Anxiety Disorder: The GAD-7. *Archives of Internal Medicine Archive* 166(10): 1092–1097.

Srnicek N (2017) *Platform Capitalism*. Polity.

Stacey A (2024) '16 nurses died by suicide during MNC's FtP process in six years', *Nursing Standard*. Available from https://rcni.com/nursing-standard/newsroom/news/16-nurses-died-suicide-during-nmcs-ftp-process-six-years-207296 [accessed 10 March 2025].

Stark D and Vanden Broeck P (2024) Principles of algorithmic management. *Organization Theory* 5(2). https://doi.org/10.1177/26317877241257213

Stein M (2000) Envy and the defences against anxiety paradigm. *Human Relations* 53(2): 193–211.

Steiner J (1993) *Psychic Retreats: Pathological Organizations in Psychotic, Neurotic and Borderline Patients*. Routledge.

Stonehouse R (2025) 'Filming me sleep on ward made my mental health worse', *BBC West Investigations*. Available from www.bbc.com/news/articles/cq8kqzgel2no [accessed 10 March 2025].

StopSIM (2023) 'StopSIM Coalition disbanding statement'. Available from https://stopsim.co.uk/2023/05/18/stopsim-coalition-disbanding-statement/ [accessed 10 March 2025].

Taylor P, Baldry C, Bain P and Ellis V (2003) 'A unique working environment': health, sickness and absence management in UK call centres. *Work, Employment and Society* 17(3): 435–458.

Taylor R (2023) 'Concern as a third of NHS mental health treatments shift online', *The Guardian*. Available from www.theguardian.com/society/2023/jul/02/concern-as-a-third-of-nhs-mental-health-treatments-shift-online [accessed 10 March 2025].

Therapy Meets Numbers (2022) When ideology meets reality. Available from https://therapymeetsnumbers.com/when-ideology-meets-reality/ [accessed 10 March 2025].

Thomas R (2024) 'Leaked NHS figures reveal 15,000 died in care of mental health trusts in one year', *The Independent*. Available from https://t.co/S7AoWUM538 [accessed 10 March 2025].

Thompson P and Laaser K (2021) Beyond technological determinism: revitalising labour process analyses of technology, capital and labour. *Work in the Global Economy* 1(1–2): 139–159.

Ticona J and Mateescu A (2018) Trusted strangers: carework platforms' cultural entrepreneurship in the on-demand economy. *New Media & Society* 20(11): 4384–4404.

Ticona J, Mateescu A and Rosenblat A (2018) *Beyond Disruption: How Tech Shapes Labor across Domestic Work & Ridehailing*. Data & Society Research Institute.

Timimi S (2019) The Flawed Ideologies of Diagnosis and IAPT. In C Jackson and R Rizq (eds) *The Industrialisation of Care: Counselling & Psychotherapy in a Neoliberal Age*. PCCS Books.

Torous J, Wisniewski H, Bird B, Carpenter E, David G, Elejalde D, et al (2019) Creating a digital health smartphone app and digital phenotyping platform for mental health and diverse healthcare needs: an interdisciplinary and collaborative approach. *Journal of Technology in Behavioral Science* 4: 73–85.

TUC (2020) 'Workers in the UK put in more than £35bn worth of unpaid overtime last year'. Available from www.tuc.org.uk/news/workers-uk-put-more-ps35-billion-worth-unpaid-overtime-last-year-tuc-analysis [accessed 10 March 2025].

TUC (2023) *Digitisation in the Public Sector: Recommendations for Union Action. A Report by the Why Not Lab for the TUC*. TUC.

Tussell (2022) *Tech Titans: The UK Public Sector's Top Technology Suppliers*. Tussell.

Umney C, Stuart M, Bessa I, Joyce S, Neumann D and Trappmann V (2024) Platform labour unrest in a global perspective: how, where and why do platform workers protest? *Work, Employment and Society*, 38(1): 3–26.

UN CRPD (United Nations Committee on the Rights of Persons with Disabilities) (2024) *Report of the Committee on the Rights of Persons with Disabilities on its Thirtieth Session* (4–22 March). UN CRPD/C/30/2.

Vallas S and Schor JB (2020) What do platforms do? Understanding the gig economy. *Annual Review of Sociology* 46: 273–294.

van Doorn N (2017) Platform labor: on the gendered and racialized exploitation of low-income service work in the 'on-demand' economy. *Information, Communication & Society* 20(6): 898–914.

van Toorn, G (2024) *United against Algorithms: A Primer on Disability-led Struggles against Algorithmic Injustice*. University of New South Wales and Cardiff University. https://doi.org/10.60836/aweg-0922

van Toorn G and Soldatić K (2024) The digital welfare state: contestations, considerations and entanglements. *Journal of Sociology* 60(3): 523–539.

Vedder R (2018) '$33,000 academic journals articles that almost no one reads', *Forbes*. Available from www.forbes.com/sites/richardvedder/2018/07/12/33000-academic-journal-articles-that-almost-no-one-reads [accessed 10 March 2025].

Vertesi J (2024) 'Don't be fooled: Much "AI" is just outsourcing, redux', *Tech Policy Press*. Available from www.techpolicy.press/dont-be-fooled-much-ai-is-just-outsourcing-redux/ [accessed 10 March 2025].

REFERENCES

Vicari S and Kirby D (2023) Digital platforms as socio-cultural artifacts: developing digital methods for cultural research. *Information, Communication & Society* 26(9): 1733–1755.

Vinge V (1993) The coming technological singularity: how to survive the post-human era. *Whole Earth Review*.

Voet L (2021) 'Trade unions take on platform companies in the struggle for decent work', *Social Europe*. Available from www.socialeurope.eu/trade-unions-take-on-platform-companies-in-the-struggle-for-decent-work [accessed 10 March 2025].

Waddell M and Kraemer S (2021) *The Tavistock Century: 2020 Vision*. Phoenix Publishing House.

Waldman A, Miller M, Eldeib D and Blau M (2024) 'Why I left the network', *ProPublica*. Available from https://projects.propublica.org/why-i-left-the-network/ [accessed 11 March 2025].

Wang S (2020) Calculating dating goals: data gaming and algorithmic sociality on Blued, a Chinese gay dating app. *Information, Communication & Society* 23(2): 181–197.

Waters S and Palmer H (2021) *Work-related Suicide: A Qualitative Analysis of Recent Cases with Recommendations for Reform*. University of Leeds.

Waters S and McKee M (2023) Ofsted: a case of official negligence? *BMJ* 381: 1147.

Watson J (ed) (2019) *Drop the Disorder: Challenging the Culture of Psychiatric Diagnosis*. PCCS Books Ltd.

Weintrobe S (2021) *Psychological Roots of the Climate Crisis: Neoliberal Exceptionalism and the Culture of Uncare*. Bloomsbury.

WHEC (Workplace Health Expert Committee) (2021) 'Work-related suicide'. Evidence review paper HSE WHEC-18.

Whitaker R (2019) *Mad in America: Bad Science, Bad Medicine and the Enduring Mistreatment of the Mentally Ill*. Basic Books.

WIE (Worker Info Exchange) (2021) *Managed by Bots: Data-Driven Exploitation in the Gig Economy*. WIE.

WIE (Worker Info Exchange) (2023) *JUST BEAT IT! How Just Eat Robo-fires its Workers*. WIE.

WIE (Worker Info Exchange) (2024) *Dying for Data: How the Gig Economy Public Data Deficit Conceals £1.9 Billion in Wage Theft, Runaway Carbon Emissions, and a Health & Safety Catastrophe*. WIE.

Williams J (2018) *Stand Out of Our Light: Freedom and Resistance in the Attention Economy*. Cambridge University Press.

Wilshire C (2019) 'ME awareness: The Pace Trial: how a debate over science empowered a whole community', *The ME Association*. Available from https://meassociation.org.uk/2019/05/me-awareness-the-pace-trial-how-a-debate-over-science-empowered-a-whole-community-09-may-2019 [accessed 10 March 2025].

Wired Insider, 'The Great Data Convergence: Where analytics meets artificial intelligence'. Available from www.wired.com/sponsored/story/the-great-data-convergence/ [accessed 10 March 2025].

Wiseman E (2021) 'Are robot therapists the future?', *The Guardian*. Available from www.theguardian.com/society/2021/aug/08/is-robot-therapy-the-future [accessed 10 March 2025].

Wolfson T, Huws U and Farrar J and Aslam Y (2022) Alongside but not in front. *Work Organisation, Labour & Globalisation* 16(1): 104–120.

Wood S, Niven K and Braeken J (2016) Managerial abuse and the process of absence among mental health staff. *Work, Employment and Society* 30(5): 783–801.

Yancher I (2022) 'Lyra health limits access to high-quality treatments "for our own good"', *Medium*. Available from https://livpsy.medium.com/lyra-health-limits-access-to-high-quality-treatments-for-our-own-good-29b7dd0138e0 [accessed 10 March 2025].

Younis T (2023) *The Muslim, State and Mind: Psychology in Times of Islamophobia*. Sage.

Zamanian K (2011) Attachment theory as defense: what happened to infantile sexuality? *Psychoanalytic Psychology* 28(1): 33–47.

Zeavin H (2021) *The Distance Cure: A History of Teletherapy*. MIT Press.

Index

A

academic publishing 91–92
Active Hope 94
adult education 92–93
advertising 16, 35, 68, 71, 82
  DigitalBFF 80–81
  standards 80, 100
AI (Artificial Intelligence) 1–3, 8, 20, 101
  AI-Mental Health and Safety (AI-MHS) 11–12, 97–99
  bad data used to develop 14
  debate on knowledge creation 90–91
  defences against thinking 16–19
  developing regulatory tools for 100
  economic potential of generative 10–11
  forms of 6
  issues and collective bargaining wins 34
  therapy chatbots 2, 3–6, 12, 21, 26–27
  using discriminatory data 12
algorithmic
  impact assessments (AIAs) 34
  management 21, 28–29, 41, 43, 45, 89, 96
  transparency 29, 30, 34, 54, 58, 60
algorithms, discrimination in 12
Amazon 9–10, 89
  Project Nessie 10
Angerland 1–19
antidepressants 9, 51, 52
anxiety
  and depression questionnaires 8–9, 43
  in psychoanalytic thinking 14, 15
  of therapists 47
App Drivers and Couriers Union (ADCU) 29
appification 5–6, 21
apps
  data breaches 11–12
  dating 69, 72, 77, 79
  Eliza2035 5, 21, 26–27
  mental health 21, 99–102
attention market 68, 69–70, 71
attrition by design 31–32, 50

austerity
  and mental health services 7, 37–38, 39, 49, 51, 61
  and welfare reform 49–51
'auto-intimacy' 18
auto-therapy 18

B

bad therapy and 'bad therapists' 14–15, 53, 65, 101
  complaints against 35, 66, 89, 96
  personal attacks on social media 74–75
Bazerman, Max 16
BBC Radio 4 48
  File on 4 35
  Today programme 99
BBC Radio 5 Live 44
benefits system 49–51
Bertillon, Alphonse 75
British Medical Journal (BMJ) 51
The Brussels Appeal 33
bullying 43, 95–96
Buolamwini, Joy 12, 101

C

call centres, therapy
  contacting 14, 22–23, 72
  IAPT and introducing idea of 39
  working in 41, 42, 45, 62, 64, 89
Case, Anne 8
Cass Review 84
CBT-Lite 2, 7, 8, 20, 52, 65
  concerns over treatment for ME/CFS 39
  recovery claims 14
  see also iCBT-Lite
Chaibi, Leïla 87–88
'Cheer up love' mental health policy 7, 49–51
Chowdhury, Rumman 101
Chun, Wendy 12
Clegg, Nick 99
Clifford, Emma 49
cognitive behavioural therapy *see* CBT-Lite; iCBT-Lite

129

commodification of therapy 2, 11, 28, 40, 68, 71–72
confidentiality and safeguarding, ethics of 70
consent, online 75
consumer ratings and rankings 15, 28, 35, 74–75, 100
Costco 98
Counsellors Together UK (CTUK) 59, 62
COVID-19 2, 13, 58, 59
critical action learning (CAL) 92–94

D

Dalal, Farhad 7, 47–48
data
  breaches 8, 11–12, 13
  colonialism 12
  privacy 11–12
  protection 75, 85, 100
  transparency 29, 54, 58, 60
Data Protection and Digital Information Bill 30
datafication 6, 21
  of despair 11–13
dating apps 69, 72, 77, 79
Deaton, Angus 8
deindustrialization of therapy 7, 11, 20, 28, 37, 71
depression
  and anxiety questionnaires 8–9, 43
  medication for 9, 51, 52
  proposed changes in guidelines for treatment of 51–52
DigitalBFF 21, 80–82
digitalization 2, 13, 21, 28
  of consulting room 70
  of trucking industry 28, 54
disability
  benefits 49, 51
  justice campaigning 94
diversity and equality initiatives in the US 98
dynamic pricing 10, 54, 60, 72, 88, 89, 97

E

Electronic Logging Devices (ELD) 28, 45
electronic performance management (EPM) 43
Eliza2035 5, 21, 26–27
Employee Assistance Programmes (EAPs) 7, 31, 32
  investigation into 35
  a new type of 100–101
  RemotelyHelpful 21, 22–24, 26
'enshittification' 14
European Commission 6, 57
European Trade Union Confederation (ETUC) 34
European Union Platform Work Directive 33–34

F

Federal Trade Commission (FTC) 8, 13, 60, 80, 82
  lawsuit against Amazon 9–10
feminization of psychotherapy 57, 61
free association, intention of 87–90
Freedom of Association and Protection of the Right to Organise Convention 33
Freire, Paulo 18, 93
Freud, David 50
Freud, Sigmund 73, 75, 78, 83
Fromm, Erich 10, 71, 72
'The Future of Therapy' survey 47

G

gambling addiction 8
Garofalo, Livia 29, 30, 54, 56, 69
Gebru, Timnit 12
Glasser, Mervin 73
'guillotine logic' 65–67

H

Hair-n-Teeth x
Hall, Wendy 99
Haugen, Frances 101
Hayes, Chris 68, 69, 71
health and safety at work 96, 97–98
Hi Sigmund™ 3–6
Huber, Linda 57
'hyper-rationality' 48

I

iCBT-Lite 2, 8, 20, 65
  concerns around safety of 47
  recovery claims 14, 50–51
  shift in NHS towards 39, 45–46
ideological capture of therapy 80, 84
Increased Access to Psychological Therapies (IAPT) programme 37–52
  austerity as policy backdrop to 37–38, 49–51
  change to guidelines for treatment of depression 51–52
  concerns over safety of using and providing 46–47
  erosion
    of diagnosis 42–43
    of supervision for therapists 43
  evidence base 38, 40, 41, 44, 46–47
  gamification of performance data 44, 45, 48
  juggernaut 38–41
  lack of oversight 40
  move to digital therapy 45–49
  Psychological Wellbeing Practitioners (PWPs) 38, 40, 41, 42, 45
  rebranded as NHS Talking Therapies 37
  recovery claims 31, 38

INDEX

services in job centres 51
 workload and working conditions 41–45
industrialization of therapy 7, 20, 28, 40–41, 43
intellectual property 90–92
intentionality 86–87
International Labour Organization (ILO) 33, 88
intimacy 78–79
 'auto' 18
 of online therapy 18, 68, 69, 70–71

K

Kassem, Sarrah 89
knowledge creation 90–92

L

Levy, Karen 5, 29, 44, 45
Lindtner, Silvia 57
litigation ix, 7, 9, 30, 80
 challenging politics of therapy 83–84
 suing therapists 9, 80–82
lived experience in mental health services 85–86

M

marketization of therapy 2, 28, 40, 68
Matrix Resurrections 13
Mattioli, Dana 2, 9–10, 29
McKinsey 5, 10
mental health activism 85–86
mental health apps 21, 99–102
 data breaches 11–12
 Eliza2035 5, 21, 26–27
Michaels, Linda 9, 78
MILF therapy 73–74
misogyny 74, 75
Money-Kyrle, Robert 17, 103
monopoly capitalism 6, 9, 40, 71–72
MuchBetterHelp 99–102
myalgic encephalomyelitis/chronic fatigue syndrome (ME/ CFS) 39

N

National Audit Office (NAO) 48
National Health Service (NHS)
 bullying in 43, 95–96
 deaths of patients in mental health facilities 85
 extraction of data 3, 37–38, 41, 46
 trade deal discussions with US on 8
 midwives 95
 NHS Direct 39
 NHS Talking Therapies 37–38, 40, 41, 52
  antidepressants vs. 51–52
  IAPT rebranded as 37
  key performance outcome measurements 44
  and politics of mental health 84

 private providers of mental health services 40
 selling NHS patient data back to 46
 therapists working in 58
 see also Increased Access to Psychological Therapies (IAPT) programme
National Institute for Health and Care Excellence (NICE) 2, 43, 51, 52
neoliberal paternalism x, 7, 28, 90, 103
neutrality of therapy 84
Noah's Arkism 65, 103

O

Oedipus Complex 73
online dating 69, 72, 77, 79
on-demand therapy 2, 8, 10, 68

P

pay, therapists' 57, 72
 industry standard rates 55
 platformization and 54–55, 56, 66–67, 82–83, 89, 101
 surveys of weekly earnings 59
 TotalRecovery 56
performance data
 'evidence base' in mental health services 38, 40, 41, 44, 46–47, 83
 gamification of 14, 32, 44, 45, 48
 and recovery rate claims 14, 31, 38, 50–51
performance management
 algorithmic tools 43
 occupational risk and link to 96
 in therapy sector 40–41, 42, 43, 47, 54, 64, 66
 tools 43
Philipson, Ilene 18, 61
Pierce, Casey 57
PIP model 93–94
platform workers
 accessing data on 58
 The Brussels Appeal 33
 expansion in numbers 61
 lack of transparency over pay 54, 60
 OHSE risks 97
 personal and professional boundaries 74–75
 protection of 30, 33
 trade unions representing 28, 29, 33–35, 88–89
 wage theft 53, 54, 57, 58–61
platformization of therapy 2, 7, 9–11, 20
 datafication of despair 11–13
 disproportionate hit on women 57–58
 dynamic pricing 10, 54, 60, 72, 88, 89, 97
 and pay 54–55, 56, 66–67, 82–83, 89, 101
 private providers of IAPT and logic of 46
 regulation 32–36, 80, 88, 89
 RemotelyHelpful 21, 22–24, 66

131

SCoPEd Framework and failure to
 address 64
TotalRecovery 21, 24–26, 55–57, 71
precarity of work 29–30, 59, 62
predatory pricing and pay systems 54, 58,
 60–61
Prescription Digital Therapeutics (PDT) 5
Pring, John 49, 50
private medical insurance 7, 29, 48, 61
 determining what counts as therapy 65
 US model 8
professional cannibalism 53, 55, 62–64
psychic pilates 37–52
psychotherapy
 detective work of 75–76
 doing deep work of 70–71, 76–79,
  103–104
 feminization of 57, 61
 postwar expansion 83
 protecting relational therapy 65–66
 two-tier system of 53, 82–83

R

rating and ranking of therapists 15, 28, 35,
 74–75, 100
Ratner, Austin 73
RealTherapy™ 19, 80–105
regulation
 of mental health apps 99–102
 of platforms and platform work 32–36, 80,
  88, 89
 of therapists 53–54, 62–63
RemotelyHelpful 21, 22–24, 66
researching apps and online platforms 21–27
retail therapy 71–72
revenge therapy 74–76
Right to Organise and Collective Bargaining
 Convention 33
Rizq, Rosemary 42, 44, 48, 66

S

Scope for Professional Education and
 Development (SCoPEd) 53–54, 59,
 62–64
self-regulation 32–36
Shestakofsky, Ben 10
Shrier, Abigail 14–15
SilverLinings 45–49
social media and therapy 68–69, 70, 71,
 74–75
social model of mental health 86–87
Srnicek, Nick 11, 28, 46
Steiner, John 78
suicide, work-related 96–97
suing therapists 9, 80–82
supervision of therapists 43, 89
Survival Surgeries 94
Surviving Work viii

T

text-based services 10, 21, 46–47, 54, 56
 being sued for questioning 80–82
 for teenagers 7–8
theraceuticals 3, 8–9
therapeutic relationships online 10, 68
 MILF therapy 73–74
 retail therapy 71–72
 revenge therapy 74–76
Therapeutic Tinder 68–79
therapists 53–67
 collective thinking and acting 66–67
 pay 54–55, 56, 57, 59, 66–67, 82–83,
  89, 101
 professional cannibalism 53, 55, 62–64
 suggestions for tackling UberTherapy 104
 suing 9, 80–82
 supervision of 43, 89
 two-tier system 53, 82–83
 wage theft and predatory pricing 58–62
 working in and alongside IAPT
  services 41–45
 see also UberTherapists
thinking
 defences against 16–19, 48
 intentional 94–95
 resisting technologies that act as defences
  against 90–95
TikTok 58, 75
TotalRecovery 21, 24–26, 71
 accessing the platform 55–57
trade unions 87–90
 action learning guides 94
 and mental health in workplace 97, 98
 organizing tools 92–93
 representing platform workers 28, 29,
  33–35, 88–89
 representing UberTherapists 88–90,
  94–95
 right to join 33
transparency
 algorithmic 29, 30, 34, 54, 58, 60
 data 29, 54, 58, 60

U

UberTherapists 28–30
 anxiety 47
 bad therapy and 'bad therapists' 14–15, 53,
  65, 101
 complaints against 35, 66, 89, 96
 personal attacks on social media 74–75
 burnout 5, 42, 47, 97
 caseloads 54, 82–83
 concerns over safety of 47
 'guillotine logic' 65–67
 pay 54–55, 56, 57, 59, 66–67, 82–83,
  89, 101
 rating and ranking of 15, 28, 74–75, 100

INDEX

selecting 70
suggestions for tackling UberTherapy 104
trade union organizing 88–90, 94–95
  in US 54
working for *TotalRecovery* 55–58
UberTherapy ix–x, 1–3, 20–36
  architecture of 20–21
  attrition by design 31–32
  business models 21
  concerns over safety of using and providing 46–47
  datafication of despair 11–13
  a defence against thinking 16–19, 48
  as an extractive industry ix, 9, 12–13, 37–38
  financial logic 37
  monopoly capitalism 6–7
  MuchBetterHelp 99–102
  political debate 65–67
  researching apps and online platforms 21–27
  rethinking business of 102–105
  sabor a mierda 13–16
  self-regulation 32–36
United States (US)
  attack on diversity and equality initiatives 98
  DigitalBFF lawsuit 80–82
  employment relations 30
  expansion of therapy 61
  private healthcare system 8
  text-based platforms 7–8
  therapy graduates 64
  UberTherapists in 54

venture capital and digital start ups 10
wage theft 58
Universal Credit 49, 50

V

venture capital 6, 10, 62

W

wage theft 53, 54, 57, 58–61
Weintrobe, Sally 17, 65, 103
welfare system 49–51
Williams, Jutta 101
women
  bullying of 95–96
  disproportionately hit by platformization 57–58
  dominating both sides of therapy relationship 57
  therapists of colour 65
Work and Health Programme 49
Worker Information Exchange (WIE) 29
working conditions
  deterioration of 66–67
  IAPT 41–45
  improving 90, 101
workplace, mental health in 95–99
World Mental Health Day 2022 48

Y

Younis, Tarek 49

Z

Zeavin, Hanna 2, 18, 78

www.ingramcontent.com/pod-product-compliance
Lightning Source LLC
Chambersburg PA
CBHW071715020426
42333CB00017B/2279